Misunderstood!

The Fast Guide to
Communicating at Work:

What to Say, How to Say It, and
When to Shut Up

Allie Casey

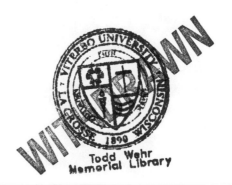

Misunderstood! The Quick Guide to Communicating at Work—
What to Say, How to Say It and When to Shut Up
ISBN 978-0-9826725-4-9
Unattributed quotations are from Allie Casey.

Allie Casey
7651 Ashley Park Court, Suite 408-144
Orlando, FL 32835
407-313-4967
info@alliecasey.com
www.AllieCasey.com

Limits of Liability and Disclaimer of Warranty

Warning – Disclaimer

How to Receive Your FREE Bonus Gifts

To receive your 3 FREE Bonus Downloads from *Misunderstood! The Fast Guide to Communicating at Work—What to Say, How to Say It and When to Shut Up* go to:

www.TheFastGuideToCommunicatingAtWork.com

BONUS #1 –
AN INSTANT PDF DOWNLOAD OF THE ENTIRE BOOK!

All the tips and techniques at your fingertips! Not sure how to tell your loud co-worker to pipe down—pull up the answer instantly!

BONUS #2 –
AN AUDIO DOWNLOAD OF ALL THE MAIN POINTS!

Five pages of the "BEST-OF-THE-BEST" highlights from every chapter in an audio format—listen when it's convenient for you. An amazing learning "listen on the go" experience in a few short minutes—packed with insights and golden nuggets!

BIG DADDY BONUS #3 –
MISUNDERSTOOD!
6 STEPS TO MOVING FROM CONTENTION
TO COMMON GROUND
60 Minute Power-Packed Teleseminar

If workplace clashes are causing you ANXIETY, then this teleseminar replay teaches you how to manage DIFFERING viewpoints and CLASHING styles so you can be your best!

Step 1 – Purchase *Misunderstood!* today, then go to www.TheFastGuideToCommunicatingAtWork.com

Step 2 – Enter your name, email and special code number and get Instant Access to your FREE Bonuses! Your book's special code is FG1CW410E1

---

www.TheFastGuideToCommunicatingAtWork.com

Get Your FREE Six-Part Audio Series
"The Power of Effective Communication"
and the Listening Skills Assessment Here

Finally, Learn 29 Proven Techniques for Creating Instant Rapport, Mastering Difficult Conversations, and Becoming a Powerful, Persuasive Communicator!

Listen to this information-packed audio series and learn:

- How to start a riveting conversation with anyone and keep it going
- Three ways to avoid misunderstandings and get your message heard
- Two kinds of questions to use to get the information you want
- Three keys to instantly determine someone's motivating style
- The single most effective technique for giving feedback and changing someone's behavior
- Five critical strategies for adapting your communication style and becoming a powerful, influential communicator
- And much, much more.

Get Instant Access to Your
FREE Six-Part Audio Series
"The Power of Effective Communication" at
www.CommunicationSkillsSuccess.com

"Open up a place in the conversation
so your listener can fit in."

~ Allie Casey

To you, courageous reader,
for having the guts to acknowledge yourself
as a party in the communication exchange and
willing to do something about it.

To my siblings — all six of you —
you have always been there for me.

Special Appreciation

*I owe a heartfelt thank-you
to Mark — your tacit support has not gone unnoticed.*

Sis — your cheers kept me focused on getting this project done.

Contents

14

Introduction

"Seek first to understand before seeking to be understood."
                                                    ~ *Dr. Stephen Covey*

In grade school, I recall watching my teacher struggle to communicate a new idea to a student who couldn't grasp the concept. What was obvious to me — he misunderstood a phrase she used — was oblivious to her. At the time, I thought I could teach my classmate better than she and cause less humiliation for him. That one incident sparked a curiosity about the dynamics of misunderstandings and an aspiration to become more attuned to others and a better communicator — a lofty goal for a very shy kid.

But eventually, I did find my passion as a professional speaker and trainer conducting programs on corporate image, service, and communication skills. It was not a straight-line career path to my calling. Along the way, I have been an entrepreneur, manager, salesperson, consultant, and coworker. I learned from all of those roles and experiences. But I learned the most from hysterical (not in a good way) audience members, angry customers, inebriated employees, workplace bullies, those I've had to fire, copious criers, and just plain liars. The aforementioned really made me step up my communication game — and they provided the real-life stories behind my articles and this book.

Though you'll find lots of solutions for sticky situations in these pages, my intention is for you to consider a different way of being with your fellow human beings and to realize that all people want from one another is to connect. I encourage you to stop, to listen, and to ponder why people might think the way they do before you attempt to get them to think the way you do. Or, as Dr. Stephen Covey put so beautifully and in fewer words, "Seek first to understand before seeking to be understood."

My hope for you is that, each time you engage in a conversation, you consider it an opportunity to deepen your understanding, listen with your heart, and learn something new. Your workplace and the world could use fewer misunderstandings and more productivity and good will.

Wishing you happy and effective conversations,

Allie Casey

How to Use This Book

U se the information in this book to address communication problems such as giving negative feedback or recovering from a misunderstanding. Use it to enhance your daily interactions with new thoughts, different approaches, and a fresh outlook on your confidence and credibility.

You can open this book to any section and find useful tips and techniques. There is no need to start at the beginning and read until the end unless that works best for you. I have grouped this compilation of articles into categories to help you find what you need quickly. You can keep this book nearby as a handy reference guide when your communication is going awry, or you can grab it for a quick refresher on how to negotiate a better deal for yourself or ask for a raise.

To make it even easier, at the beginning of each section I have inserted a handy checklist of salient points. I won't be offended if you rip out those pages and paste them on your cubicle wall — it is good to keep reminders and a bit of inspiration where you can see it.

Expect overlap as you read through the sections. That's okay — repetition helps us learn. If you don't get the message in one article, you might get your "aha" in another. And remember to get your FREE six-part audio series, "The Power of Effective Communication," at www.CommunicationSkillsSuccess.com.

"Be more concerned with your character than with your reputation.
Your character is what you really are while your reputation
is merely what others think you are."

~ Dale Carnegie

Confidence
Credibility
Connection

"Communication — it's not just the words."

Section 1 – Salient Points

☑ Polish your soft skills because everything you do, you do with and through other people.

☑ Connect with someone today with your full attention. Listen to a coworker without offering a solution. Just be present.

☑ Be confident — it's the first thing people notice about you. It's the energy that tells the world you are self-assured.

☑ Credibility is the sense and proof of believability you portray to others.

☑ Connection is critical. People do business with people they like, so be likeable.

☑ The more self-assured you are, the bigger your sphere of influence.

☑ Take responsibility for communicating effectively and you'll earn respect.

☑ Model what you expect from others.

Plays Well with Others

Simply put, soft skills are our ability to get along with others. Good soft skills connect us with each other. Poor skills can turn a simple misunderstanding into a bewildering war. Okay, I'm painting with a broad stroke here, but you get my point — learning to play well with others makes it easier to live with others.

Soft skills are the bundle of personality traits -- dependability, conscientiousness, friendliness -- that characterize your relationship with other people. Think of the cell phone commercial featuring a customer with his service team behind him. That team represents all the skills you need to ensure that you stay linked together. And staying connected is the key to everything you hope to accomplish in this world.

Why? Because everything you do, you do with or through other people.

Much like Robert Fulghum's book, *Everything I Know I Learned in Kindergarten*, or Dale Carnegie's *How to Win Friends and Influence People*, the principles are simple. The execution is not always so easy.

A quick review of Fulghum's lessons learned reveals the simplicity of his axioms. Consider these:

- Share everything.
- Play fair.
- Say you're sorry when you hurt somebody.
- When you go out into the world, hold hands and stick together.

Sage advice. Dale Carnegie clearly understood the hard impact of soft skills. His words of wisdom:

- Be interested in others.
- Find common ground.
- Make the other person feel important.
- Smile and use people's name.

Again — simple.

Yes, tweeting and blogging and online social networking allow you to "connect" with lots of people. But do you really know the 12,847 people you "friended?"

Try connecting with someone and giving them your full attention today. Pick up the phone and have a conversation. Listen to a coworker without offering a solution. Look your child in the eye. Give your undivided attention to your partner. Smile with sincerity at the guy that bags your groceries.

Connect in a way that makes a difference. Be present — it's a gift to a fellow human. That's why soft skills are important.

Confidence — The Best Nonverbal Communication

Confidence is often the first thing we notice about someone. We might think it is our body parts that get attention (and sometimes that's true) but confidence has more impact. Confidence is the energy that tells the world you are self-assured and self-reliant. Good communicators are confident communicators.

Confidence is not arrogance. Arrogance is about self-importance, whereas confidence is about making others feel important while retaining a high level of self-respect.

Confidence is the message that says "I'm competent, capable, and poised." Confidence is not limited to age or position. I have seen confident eight-year-olds — and if you have ever been on a ski slope you know what I'm talking about. A sense of overall confidence keeps you going when faced with challenges.

Confidence is having full trust in yourself to act on your own behalf. This does not mean you need to know all the answers; it means you know when to seek answers and listen openly.

Try these tips when you find your confidence flagging before a big presentation or when facing a difficult conversation:
- **Know your material.** If you suffer from situational timidity that deflates your confidence, your best defense is to know your subject matter. A pending presentation, speech, or diffi-

cult conversation that is challenging your self-assurance is best managed by knowing as much about the situation or topic as possible. Nothing says confidence like knowing your stuff.

- **Admit you don't know.** No, this doesn't contradict the first piece of advice. Rather, it says, "I am smart enough to know I don't know everything." Only arrogance supposes complete knowledge. Being willing to learn sends a very powerful and confident message.

- **Take more risks.** Step out of your self-imposed boundaries and take on a project, a course, or a situation that feels slightly uncomfortable. No risk means no opportunity to experience growth, and confident people are always growing.

- **Be coachable.** Confident people open up the lines of communication and practice active listening. Be willing to make changes, listen to other solutions, and entertain all possibilities.

- **Don't worry about what others think** but do have some insight into how others perceive you. Confident people choose to understand how they appear to the world, and they choose to accept it or change it. But they don't worry about what others think.

Powerful communication begins before you speak. Let your confidence do the talking.

Five Mistakes that
Crush Self-Confidence

Self-confidence is a key characteristic of successful communicators. Confidence, or the ability to rely on yourself, is reflected in your interpersonal skills, your appearance, your posture, and your voice.

Whether you are engaging a potential client, introducing yourself at a function, or answering the phone, your level of ease and self-assurance will determine your success at building relationships, persuading others, and negotiating.

Consider these five mistakes that sabotage self-confidence:

1. **Failing to relax.** Tension and stress in your body often result in a pinched voice and a stiff-shouldered posture. Proper breathing is your best foundation; without it, you don't stand a chance of portraying effortless poise. Relax your neck, upper back, and shoulders frequently throughout the day.

2. **Apologizing for anything you are about to do or say.** Never say, "I'm new at this," or "I'm a little nervous," or any statement that reflects negatively on you, especially when you are giving a presentation. Your body reflects what you are thinking, and negative self-evaluation is not part of the confident person's language.

3. **Listening to negative feedback immediately after a presentation.** If you are new to taking the lead in a meeting, giving a speech for the first time, or presenting a new idea to the executive committee, refrain from listening to negative feedback immediately after your big moment. Here's why — no matter how wonderful 95 percent of your presentation was, you'll only hear the one thing that went wrong. It's an instant confidence-killer. Soak in the feeling of a job well done and then listen to what you can do better next time.

4. **Not wearing comfortable and appropriate clothing.** If you are uncomfortable because your pants bind, your jacket restricts your movement, your shirt won't stay tucked in, or you are worried about being too casually dressed for the occasion, you are not going to feel confident. Proper fit is when there is enough air between you and your clothing that allows you to move comfortably — not too much, not too little. As far as appropriateness goes, aim to be a bit more "dressed" than your audience — even if you're talking to an audience of one.

5. **Not doing your homework.** You know that icky feeling you got when you didn't study for the test? You're not in school anymore. Prepare, check your facts, and bring plenty of No. 2 pencils. Know your objectives, your speech, and your product or service inside out. Don't mistake this for thinking you have to know everything. Always be willing to learn, but don't fake knowing your stuff.

The more self-assured you are, the bigger your sphere of influence will be.

How to Manage the Three Levels of Credibility

Credibility is the sense and proof of believability you portray to others. You must appear credible before your words can be heard as valuable. Therefore, credibility is a critical component of good communication.

Understanding the different types of credibility will help you create and maintain a positive impression before and after meeting someone. You will want to monitor your credibility as it ebbs and flows through the communication process.

Here are the three levels of credibility and how you can use them to gain respect and have more influence:

Initial – This is credibility that precedes you. It is formed by what others say, read, and hear about you. It is your reputation, and you create it by your education, title, training, and writing. Today's instant messaging mediums and news creation (as opposed to news reporting) means others can influence how people see you.

Refusing to play in the electronic communication arena does not mean you will escape the effects of it. Not engaging sends the message that you are not up-to-date, you are hiding something, or that you have no influence in your field of work.

Here's what to do:

Monitoring your electronic reputation is critical. Use good sense, awareness, and caution when using social media. Keep business communication and social banter with friends separate. As far as possible, know who is connected to you. Remember that everything is forever on the web.

Use your resume, business cards, web sites, books, and other marketing materials to convey the message that you are of good character, charitable, and trustworthy. Create a sense of respect beforehand.

Derived – This is the credibility that is created during face-to-face communication. This type of credibility has a dynamic flow. A single word, a gesture, or your tone of voice can shift how you are perceived and believed. When your presentation does not match your reputation, your credibility begins to fade. Keep in mind that it is more difficult to recover from a poor reputation than it is to correct a good one that has gone off track.

Here's what to do:

Have a sense of how others perceive you. If you have worked hard to create a positive reputation, follow through with your posture, voice, gestures, dress, mannerisms, and verbal communication. Use all of these elements to bolster your self-confidence. Confidence is inspiring and appealing. Cultivate self-confidence but avoid arrogance. Use humor when appropriate.

Terminal – Terminal credibility is not a disease; rather, it is what you leave behind — a legacy without the death part. What will others say when you leave the room? What feelings will you impart — a sense of good will and positivity or a sense of doubt and uncertainty?

Here's what to do:

Check your perceptions. Ask for feedback and become acutely aware of how you are appearing to others. Follow up by doing what you say you will do.

Put your credibility to work for you — don't leave it to chance. Remember that what you do and communicate outside of the workplace can have an impact on your credibility in the workplace. Monitor your social media, your actions, and your words.

Five Key Questions to Ask Yourself
If You're Always Eating Lunch Alone

Effectively communicating in the workplace requires your ability to connect with and get along with others. People do business with people they like — so be likeable. You may feel that people don't like you if you don't connect with your team, if you have unusual behavior traits that put off your boss, or if you struggle to fit in with your coworkers.

It might be argued that, if people don't like you, it is their problem, not yours. This statement may be partly correct, but without taking responsibility for recognizing that you are a party in the matter, you may find yourself eating lunch alone for the balance of your career.

If you feel alienated by others, it might be time to ask yourself some difficult questions. The answers will help you gain some perspective and establish whether or not you are part of the problem. Be prepared to be brutally honest with yourself.

What evidence do you have that makes you think that people don't like you? Write down your observations. Notice any patterns in the way others react to you. Have you consistently been passed over for promotions or lost jobs because "you didn't fit in"? The key here is to determine if this really is about any one person or if you are having a challenge connecting and acting appropriately for your position. Do you make the attempt to engage others? Are you socially inept?

Do you know how to create rapport? When you speak with people do you match volume, pitch, and pace? Do you say things that cause others to react negatively or recoil? Do you stand too close or too far away when speaking to others? Do you respond appropriately to questions? Do you interrupt conversations with self-serving comments or comments unrelated to the topic? Do you interject with unsolicited advice? Are you a contrarian? Answering these questions takes a degree of self-awareness.

Are you appropriately groomed and attired for your workplace? A disheveled appearance can send a negative message — incompetent, insecure, untrustworthy — not the qualities others want to be associated with. Inappropriate dress includes clothing that fits poorly, skirts that are too short, pants that sit too low, or attire that is too casual or too dressy for the job. Do you have body odor or bad breath? Seek the help of an image consultant who can help you see yourself in a new light.

Do you know how to do your job? Do you pull your weight, or do you slack off and hope no one notices? Are you a tattletale, hoping to garner favor from your boss? Do you fail to help out your coworkers? Are you a team player?

Are you the office flirt? Do you harass coworkers or direct reports verbally? Are you a bully, or do you let others walk all over you? Do you make sexually suggestive comments or gestures? Are you too touchy-feely? Are you just plain creepy?

Consider shifting your behavior a bit. I'm not suggesting you put on a mask or pretend to be someone you are not. I am proposing that self-awareness and self-development will allow you to communicate more effectively with others. If you find yourself answering yes to more than a few of these questions, get some help. Life is too short and work days are too long to spend them being miserable.

Five Ways to Help Me Hear You

Communicating to be heard in the workplace can be different than communicating at home with family and friends. Yet too frequently we bring the patterns of familial conversations into the business environment, expecting them to work.

Make it easy for others to hear you and listen to your ideas with these five communication tips:

1. **Know Your Intention.**
   What behavior do you want from your listener as a result of your message? Do you want him or her to implement instructions? Are you seeking sympathy? Is there a behavior or habit you want this person to stop doing? Are you looking for answers to a question or solutions to a problem?

   Too frequently people couch their intentions with indirect language, hoping the message will somehow get across to the recipient. Maybe this is how you communicate with your spouse or partner, but clear and honest intention is critical to avoiding misunderstandings in the workplace.

2. **Communicate in a logical pattern.**
   This can be a challenge for circular or random thinkers as their message may only be heard by those with the same pattern of thinking — and then, maybe not!
   People prefer to receive messages in a logical format (even

random thinkers). Take a moment to format your message rather than speak your thoughts as they come to you. Family members may be forgiving of your "all over the place" conversations, but coworkers or clients may not.

3. **Avoid shorthand messages.**
   Clean up your jargon, lingo and abbreviations. Even coworkers may get lost as they struggle to translate an alphabet soup of industry jargon or personal shorthand. While your listener is trying to recall what "PTI interface in the QRS protocol" is, he has lost the context of the message. Clean it up if you want to be heard.

4. **Remove the roadblocks to receiving your message.**
   Distractions are a major cause of misunderstandings in a conversation. Help your listener by removing all obstacles blocking the path of your message. You won't be able to control internal filters such as mental or emotional instability, but you can be aware of physical distractions such as illness, hunger, or fatigue if you're observant, present, and aware. Obvious anxiety or fear can be lessened by letting your listener know that you are aware of those emotions.

   Help remove language barriers by speaking clearly, enunciating, and avoiding excess words. Move to a different location if noise or visual distractions are present.

5. **Communicate in the way your listener likes to communicate.**
   A quick observation can shed light on how your listener likes to receive information. Do you need to create rapport first? Would a written note facilitate your verbal message? Will they only want to hear the bottom line without a laundry list of details? Don't bore your listener by giving too much information if they have little tolerance for such. Conversely, don't skip over information that would be critical for them to make an informed decision.

Getting your message across so it is heard in the way you intended takes more than blurting out a few sentences. Step into the shoes of your listener and communicate from their point of view if you want them to hear your ideas or opinions. Take responsibility for communicating effectively, and your listener will respond favorably and treat you with more respect.

Power Up Your Message - Five Ways to Use Nonverbal Communication

Your nonverbal communication is more powerful than your words when the two are not aligned. If you want your words to be more influential and to carry more weight and authority, then you must make certain your nonverbal message is congruent with your verbal message.

Here are five ways to use your nonverbal communication more effectively:

1. In low-risk conversations, your nonverbal message (i.e., your body language and the sound of your voice) naturally supports your words. You sparkle, smile, and stand straighter when you're elated, and you slump and frown when you are not. But there are times when you want to appear confident when you are not feeling confident. If you ignore your body and voice, relying only on your words, your body will betray you every time. To match the two, breathe from your belly, straighten your back, and relax your jaw. This prevents your voice from sounding pinched and your body from appearing timid. This posture will send a positive message to your mind and you will begin to feel as confident as your words.

2. Consider the nonverbal message you send when you are listening to others. Is your face betraying your smile? You can fake a smile, but your eyes and facial muscles will tell on you. If you want others to be interested in you, then you need to

41

sincerely be interested in others. Consciously decide to be fully aware and present, and your nonverbal message will follow suit.

3. Beware of nervous and distracting habits that dilute your intention. Finger-picking, face-touching, or jangling coins in your pockets will divert attention away from your message. Some habits are so ingrained that you won't notice them unless they are pointed out. Ask for feedback or coaching to catch these communication-killers.

4. Practice using gestures to enhance the important points you are trying to make. Watch yourself in a mirror to avoid unnatural movements such as moving your arms as though they were attached to your waist, or flailing or distracting hand movements. You are aiming for balanced and natural motion, not overly rehearsed gestures to support your words.

5. Emotions are tricky to manage and can often get the best of us in difficult conversations. Use your breath, count to ten, or release your emotions before your encounter. If you must take a break to regain composure during a challenging or emotionally charged conversation, request it before you completely break down. If you have a few moments beforehand, practice this exercise: Place your arms out from your body in an aiming position, hands clasped and pointing. Now trace a lazy eight figure in a sweeping side-to-side motion with your arms. This will help balance and connect the emotional and logical sides of your brain. In emotional situations, the right (emotional) brain is firing rapidly. This exercise works well before giving a presentation, asking for a raise, or confronting a workplace bully.

Use these tips to become more influential, credible, and confident. Managing your nonverbal communication requires self-awareness — perhaps the key component of a good communicator.

Why Should I Believe You?

Trust in the workplace, trust in leadership, and connecting with others were the key phrases I found in a recent online search for "best selling business books." It's a sign of the times. A lack of leadership and trustworthiness in the workplace appears to be the norm.

Leadership is something that everyone in the workplace can practice — not just CEOs and business owners. Communicating trustworthiness starts with honest intention and self-awareness. Additionally, you can not be an effective communicator or leader if you do not provoke trust in others.

Here are five strategies for developing leadership and establishing trust:

1. **Tell the truth.** Easy to say — difficult to practice. Yet truth is what your customers, coworkers, employees, shareholders, and vendors want from you. Whether it is late deliveries, quality problems, or low earnings, you need to be honest about it. Most people CAN handle the truth. Truth requires no managing or memorization. Tell the truth — it's easier.

2. **Take forward action.** Leadership means evaluating the available information and moving onward. The best leaders make difficult and timely decisions with about 70 to 80 percent of

the information. You may never get all the details, and waiting to act may result in tragedy. Evaluate and be proactive.

3. **Do what you say you are going to do.** Okay, this may be a combination of the first two strategies, but it bears its own heading. Both actions and inactions influence others. If you promise to return a call, handle a matter, or show up on time, follow through.

4. **Be consistent.** Leadership requires consistency in behavior, mood, and language both at home and at work. Nothing kills trust like incongruence between what you do and say to one person and what you do and say to another. Treat the fast food server the same as the CEO of an organization.

5. **Be the example.** Model what you expect from others. Don't ask others to do something you wouldn't do. Trust is developed when you live according to your ethics.

Leaders appear at every level of an organization from the support team to sales to the CEO. Communicating leadership requires an inner confidence and an outer personality that can convey that confidence to others through words and actions. Many leaders possess the self-confidence to perform tasks and reach goals, but lack the ability to connect with people. Leadership and trustworthiness are earned through communication, not just results.

"To effectively communicate
we must realize that we are all different in the way
we perceive the world and use this understanding as a guide
to our communication with others."

~ Anthony Robbins

Intention
Information
Interpretation

"Tension changes how people react —
choose empathy over anger as your response."

Section 2 – Salient Points

☑ Use the "Invitation for Communication" Model: Intention>Information>Interpretation>Interaction>Integration

☑ Remember that not everyone thinks the same way you do.

☑ Perception check — is your message visually, vocally, and verbally congruent?

☑ Listening is not a passive activity — it takes awareness and perception. Listen with empathy and without assumptions.

☑ Become a leader, no matter your role or position.

☑ Create a mindset that releases you from being right and allows you the opportunity to learn.

☑ Master the art of asking the right questions.

☑ Assertively standing up for your rights is mature behavior.

☑ To influence others, shift from weak phrases to positive, assertive statements.

☑ Learn to interpret intonation, volume, pitch, rate of speech, gestures, and words from the speaker's point of view.

The 'Invitation for Communication'

What is it about communication in the workplace that invites challenge instead of cooperation? Is it ego, fear, ignorance, culture, or human nature? I can hear you checking off all of those factors and maybe adding a few of your own. But, the question remains — what can you do about decreasing misunderstandings at work?

Short of listing all the potential dreaded-conversation scenarios and a list of all the possible comebacks, I want to invite you to explore another approach: an "Invitation for Communication."

The **"Invitation for Communication"** is both a formula and a mindset. The approach is to look at a conversation as an invitation to join in and share an experience. If I invite you to an event, a party, or out on a date, you might picture a ceremony, festivities, or a romantic evening. You also have the option to accept or decline my invitation. Either way, I expect a response.

If you decline my invitation to communicate, you have agreed to disagree, in business parlance. If you accept, you agree to engage in a dialogue. Of course, if I don't hear back from you, that sets off another round of miscommunications.

The invitation also comes with the notion that there will be an exchange of some kind. If I invite you to dinner and upon your arrival I hand you a fishing rod and bait, you might get dinner in the end (or not), but I suspect that catching dinner was not what you had in mind. My thoughts did not translate into your thoughts.

And that is the objective for many workplace conversations — to get me thinking the same way that you do. When you fail to confirm that your message has been interpreted the way you intended, that's the start of another communication miscue.

The formula for the "invitation" looks like this:

Intention: What outcome do you want as a result of your message? Be honest about your intentions.
Information: This is the message.
Interpretation: This is how your listener deciphers the message.
Interaction: This is the key component — engaging to confirm the interpretation.
Integration: The intended result, change, or behavior is understood, implemented, and assimilated.
In-Time: "Too little, too late" is a formula for failure.

Use the invitation to change the way you think about engaging with others — think guest, not competitor. And use the formula as a simple way to keep on track and ensure that you have been heard correctly.

How to Make Sure Interpretation Matches Intention

Misunderstandings occur when the interpretation of a message is different from the message sender's intention. With all the possible barriers to clear communications, including personality clashes, age, gender gaps, lingo, physical well-being — not to mention content and context — it's a wonder any communication takes place at all.

Both speaker and listener can do their part to ensure that intention matches interpretation:

1. **Be clear about your purpose for communicating.** Will you be giving a directive or a set of instructions? Are you asking for feedback or an explanation? Do you want the listener to take a specific action? State your purpose in the message. "This procedure replaces the current one effective immediately." Or, "I want your thoughts on this before you leave." If you are the listener and you are confused about the purpose of the message, then ask.

2. **Give information in the way your listener likes to receive information.** Be responsible for how your message lands. You can control that. You can't be in control of the listener's response. If they prefer details first followed by the big picture, don't give them the big picture followed by the details. This takes observation and awareness.

If you are the listener, ask for the information in another format if you need it. Sometimes just asking, "Could you rephrase that?" helps. Sometimes you might need a sketch or written instructions. It is similar to giving directions — some people want the landmarks and some people want the distance.

3. **Ask for a summary.** Again, both the listener and the message sender can take on this responsibility. If you stop someone on the street to ask for directions, you would never hesitate to confirm what you heard. "You said to get back on Route 9, go about two miles, and make the first left after the four-way stop. Then I go a quarter mile and make a right. Correct?" If you need landmarks, ask, "What will I see before the first turn?"

    In the above example, the listener is confirming his interpretation. But just as easily, the direction-giver could ask for a recap by saying, "Give that back to me so I know I gave it to you correctly." This is critical; otherwise, your listener ends up in the wrong place.

    Always ask for a summary, but keep your intention for this feedback very clear — avoid making your listener feel stupid. You want the feedback to confirm you have done a good job of communicating your message and intention. The payoff of confirming your message benefits both parties — you won't have to repeat yourself, and your listener won't waste time and energy on the wrong actions.

Understanding hasn't occurred just because you spoke. Take the onus for completing the communication circle.

Six Skills You Can't Ignore If You Want to Be a Better Communicator

Communication starts before you begin speaking. If you find that you are frequently misunderstood, then it is time you take a look at yourself to find the problem. Sending clear messages takes more than spewing out a few sentences and hoping for the best.

Six Skills to Master if You Want to Be a Better Communicator:

1. **Are you sending a clear message?** Is your message organized? Do you say what you mean or are you skirting an issue by talking around it? There is a time and place for indirect communication, but when giving directions, instructions, or asking for a specific action, it is best to be direct.

   Skill: Practice asking for what you want in short, clearly stated sentences. "Joe, in order for us to meet our deadline, I'll need your report by 3 p.m. so I have time to complete my part of the project." Refrain from saying "as soon as possible," as this means something different for everyone.

2. **Can you be heard?** Is your volume loud enough? Or are you mumbling or turning your head away from your listener? Have you made an attempt to see if you have been heard and understood?

   Skill: Practice looking directly at the person you're speaking to. Make eye contact and articulate clearly with proper enunciation. Speak loudly enough to be heard. If you lack insufficient volume, practice this exercise: In a space at least 15 feet long, stand in one corner facing your partner with about 6 feet between you. Your goal is to push your partner diagonally across the room with your voice. Instruct your partner to move ONLY when they feel the volume of your voice moving him or her across the room. If your voice drops, your partner moves toward you and if there is no discernable change in volume, your partner remains in place. Practice until you can easily move your partner across the room. This is the volume level you want to practice. It will probably feel very loud at first, so ask for feedback.

3. **Do you use jargon, lingo, ten-dollar words, or text talk that is meaningless to your listener?** These habits not only cause misunderstandings, but they are also rude.

   Skill: Practice speaking in the same language as your listener. Refrain from using alphabet soup terminology or using a vocabulary above your audience. This is an easy communication snafu to untangle if you listen to yourself. Practice by recording a week's worth of phone calls, especially to customers and vendors.

4. **Have you considered how each receiver might be filtering your message?** Is there a language barrier? Do they have a different cultural background, religion, education, or position? Are they emotionally stable? Are they distracted by a headache or other ailment? Do they like you?

   Skill: Practice observing each listener for signs of confusion. Check to see if your message will pass through the receiver's filters and still be understood as you intended. Pause and give them time to process, and then verify by periodically asking them what questions they may have — don't wait until the end of the conversation if you have any doubts about their interpretation.

5. **Is your message visually, verbally and vocally congruent?** Does your body say one thing while you speak something else? Does your voice negate your words? This is the percep-

tion test. If all three parts of your communication do not align, then the message that your body language and your voice sends will always outweigh your words.

Skill: To practice this skill, you can videotape your conversations and then watch them with the sound off. Observe your body language. What message does it convey? Then watch again with the sound to see if the words and tone match your gestures. Does your head shake no when you say yes? Does your posture say, "I don't want to be here," but your words say, "Glad I came"?

6. **Have you checked your timing?** Have you consciously or unconsciously picked an inappropriate time to have a conversation? Is your listener prepared to hear what you have to say? Are you managing distractions? If you truly want to have meaningful conversations, pick the time and location wisely.

   Skill: Practice by deliberately choosing the location and time for your next challenging conversation. Avoid hallway or over the cubicle wall "by the way" bombshells. Perform difficult or sensitive discussions face-to-face in a quiet location. If you must conduct a serious conversation by phone, give your listener fair warning and the opportunity to find a private location. Avoid a text message for delicate conversations at all costs.

Communication is the responsibility of both parties. As the message sender, you must do an excellent job of conveying your intention and checking for comprehension and understanding. As the listener, check your perception and paraphrase what you have heard to avoid misunderstandings.

Communicating with the Characters in Your Workplace

Communicating at work can often resemble a sitcom where coworkers are characters and the story is driven by misunderstandings. Communicating with these characters (I mean coworkers) can be frustrating unless you know more about what makes them tick.

The good news is that your coworkers may be as identifiable as the characters in any good story. Once you get to know them, you can anticipate a certain amount of predictable behavior. Learning how to talk to these characters (or style types) will help you get your point across more effectively so that cooperation becomes the norm rather than the exception.

No matter what name you give to each style type (I use Methodicals, Expansives, Agreeables, and Governors), a distinct set of behaviors can be recognized. Master an understanding of these distinctions and shift your approach, and your chances of getting cooperation increase.

Here's what you'll need to know:

1. **What motivates them?** Mastering a keen sense of what motivates each of your coworkers gives you the greatest opportunity to communicate effectively. Each style type has priorities: keeping peace, interaction, the process, or the bottom-line.

2. **What do they seek?** Don't assume others desire the same things you do. You'll need to master an understanding of

what others desire. Do they look for attention, precision, efficiency, or acknowledgment?

3. **What do they fear?** Mastering the subtle differences here will allow you to craft your approach and message accordingly. Do they fear disagreement, humiliation, or a loss of power or stature?

4. **What is important to them?** An understanding of what each style type needs to know before moving ahead, making a decision, or listening to a suggestion is critical. Is it important for them to know how it will affect them individually, elevate their position, plausibly make sense, or provide results? Turn what's important for them into benefits if you seek cooperation or agreement.

5. **How do they behave under stress?** Tension can change how people respond to you. Master a sense of empathy. The ability to communicate empathetically has never been more important than in today's workplace. You'll need to know what behavior might show up when they are under stress. Will it be acquiescence, sarcasm, avoidance, or aggression? Don't let this behavior change your approach, except to highlight what it is they seek in the first place.

Have a little fun with this exercise. Once you notice the patterns (e.g., Methodicals feel stress when projects are not presented in a logical format or Agreeables desire cooperation and efficiency), you will be able shift your approach more quickly. More cooperation, quicker decisions, a willingness to collaborate, and fewer headaches will be your rewards.

Are You a Responsive or a Reactive Listener?

Your ability to listen and respond powerfully can radically change the quality of your personal or professional relationships. And relationships are the foundation for success in life.

"Communication is a skill that you can learn ... If you're willing to work at it, you can rapidly improve the quality of every part of your life."

~ Brian Tracy

Most people think they're good listeners. And most can't tell the difference between being a reactive listener or one who listens empathically to the speaker's message before responding. Listening is not a passive activity. It takes awareness and perception.

Responsive listeners are rewarded with consensus, understanding, and loyalty. Reactive listeners need to work much harder to be heard, and they wonder why they often feel misunderstood. So what's the difference between a responsive listener and a reactive one?

Here are five distinctions to determine what kind of listener you are:

- Reactive listeners anticipate what a speaker is going to say.
- Responsive listeners let the speaker finish and encourage more information.

59

- Reactive listeners ignore or pay little heed to nonverbal clues.
- Responsive listeners pay attention to whether words are consistent with intonation and body language.

- Reactive listeners are inflexible.
- Responsive listeners go with the flow.

- Reactive listeners are impatient.
- Responsive listeners pay attention even if the speaker is difficult to understand or hard to follow.

- Reactive listeners have an agenda.
- Responsive listeners listen with an open mind. They receive all of the information first and then, after clarification, respond to the speaker.

How powerful are your listening skills? If you see yourself in any of the reactive statements above, try becoming a more mindful listener. Make your next conversation speaker-focused and tailor your response accordingly.

Take responsibility for becoming a first-class listener and watch the quality of your relationships change.

'Where Were You on the Night in Question?' Asking the Right Kinds of Questions

Effective communicators know how to ask the right questions at the right time. Mastering the art of asking the right questions will help you gather information, build stronger relationships, let others know you are listening, and establish yourself as a leader.

To become a successful communicator, you'll need to understand the power of asking the right questions and seamlessly incorporating them into your conversations.

Here are four types of questions to ask and when to use them:

1. **Closed-ended questions prompt a single definitive answer.** Yes or no. If that is all the information you need, then this is an effective type of question to ask. Yes or no questions are best used when asking for a simple decision. "Will you be attending the meeting?" is a good example of a closed-ended question. But if you are seeking more information and you continue asking close-ended questions, your conversation will quickly become an interrogation.

2. **Open-ended questions require more than a yes or no answer.** Open-ended questions encourage dialogue and are an effective way to obtain information even from the most closed-mouthed individuals. Begin these questions with

"what" or "how" to encourage a more expansive answer. "Tell me more" is one of the most effective phrases you could incorporate into your communication. "Tell me more" promotes further conversation, indicates listening and interest, supports relationships, and decreases misunderstandings. These three words might be the most powerful yet least used words in the workplace. The easiest way to get information is to say, "Tell me more about...(a project, a process, a job function, an expected outcome, a vision, or a concept)."

3. **The third type of question is a clarifying question.** Clarifying questions are used when you are unclear about what was said. "Did you say Anne or Angie will head up the project?" This type of question can also help you make distinctions concerning the intentions and context of a message. These questions do not imply agreement or disagreement, just clarification.

4. **Finally, there are funnel questions.** These questions are effective when used with individuals that require some prompting to engage in conversation. Begin by asking a broad open-ended question. If you haven't gotten the information you need, then move on to a more specific question: "What was the response to the new product?" Continue to ask specific questions until you obtain the information you seek.

Successful communicators use questions effectively because they are calm, respectful, and genuinely interested in the answers.

Passive, Aggressive, Assertive — Oh, My!

Assertive behavior is the dynamic balance between aggressive and passive conduct. Maintaining this balance is crucial for managing relationships and standing up for your rights. Understanding and using assertive behavior is a critical business communication skill.

Imagine a scale where one side is labeled aggression and the other is labeled passive. Assertiveness indicates the midway point between the two. Move too far toward the aggressive end and your behavior might be viewed as abusive. Lean too far toward the passive side and your conduct might suggest you have no backbone.

Standing up for your rights assertively is mature behavior and it contributes to a balanced work environment. Assertive communication says you have a healthy sense of yourself and regard others as equals.

Assertive behavior does not violate the right of others to be heard, nor does it violate your own right to express yourself. Aggressive behavior is bully behavior. Every workplace seems to have at least one destructive player who feels the need to win over everything else.

When encountering an aggressive personality, it is best to remember that this person is operating from fear. This is a good time to don your Teflon® coat to keep any personal attack from sticking. If you are constantly being interrupted while you are making a point, it is acceptable to take back the stage to finish your statement. Saying something such as, "Let me finish my point, John," in a calm, steady, well-modulated voice is an acceptable technique. Repeat as needed. This pegs you as having the voice of reason and leadership.

If you are the aggressor, it would be wise to examine the results of your behavior as well as your motives. Do others avoid you? Are coworkers reluctant to support your point of view? You might be gaining the upper hand in some situations, but at what cost? What are you afraid of losing if you allow others their right to an opposing opinion?

Passive behavior as a communication style can be just as damaging — to you as well as to others. It indicates low self-esteem (as does aggressive behavior), it expects others to guess your thoughts and motives, and it slows down productivity. At first glance, a passive employee may seem ideal — he does his work and doesn't say much. What is missing from that equation is the possibility of better ideas and solutions to problems. Passive communication creates guesswork on the part of others, and it invites aggressive responses.

If you are prone to passive behavior, consider asserting yourself in low-risk situations. Give your opinion on a light-hearted but controversial topic during a lunchtime break. Adding your opinion about who is going to win American Idol or the World Series rarely causes more than playful banter while adding color to the conversation. From there, practice taking more risks by asserting yourself at meetings, even if it is only to agree with others. Your voice is important. You have the same rights as others, and letting people violate those rights contributes to a bully-driven workplace.

Should you encounter a passive communicator, help him or her by encouraging independent thought and refusing to take "I don't care what we do" or "it doesn't matter to me" as answers.

Assertive communication allows for fair exchange, collaboration, and teamwork. Assertive behavior from everyone creates a productive and pleasant workplace.

The Six Absolutely Essential Assertive Communication Techniques

Being heard in the workplace requires assertive communication skills that allow you to express yourself clearly without misunderstandings and still earn respect. Assertive does not mean loud, angry, or irritated. And respect is not synonymous with agreement; it means expressing proper concern and courtesy.

Here are six assertive communication techniques that you can practice when you want to be heard without being misunderstood:

1. **Self-disclosure** is revealing information about yourself that allows others to respond to you by creating a shared or relatable vulnerability. This is particularly difficult for managers and leaders to practice, as sharing personal deficiencies — no matter how common or insignificant — are discouraged.

    "I don't know much about ..." is a powerful statement which suggests that your willingness to learn is greater than your need to be right.

2. **The "feel, felt, found" approach** can also be an effective self-disclosure technique:

    "I understand how you feel. I felt that way myself when the company changed hands, but then as I listened to their point of view, I realized we had many common values."

3. **Acknowledging without agreeing** is another communication skill that assertive people practice. This is especially helpful when dealing with a dissenter during a meeting or presentation.

   "What an interesting thought ..." acknowledges the speaker without encouraging further conversation.
   "That might be true, and here are my thoughts ..." is another option.

4. **Calm repetition** of certain words is a communication skill that is useful when giving information that might not be well-received.

   "My intention is to provide you with the details of the new program ..." is one possible phrasing which should be clearly stated in a firm but calm voice repeatedly until you are acknowledged and given the platform.

5. **Negative affirmation** is a bit trickier to use and requires a neutral tone of voice. Occasionally someone may attempt to prove you wrong, especially regarding principles. You might try this:

   "Let me understand: are you saying I'm wrong?" Again, a calm, nonaccusatory voice is important.

6. **Repeat the negative comment** when a criticism has been directed at you without explanation. Assertively ask for more information while repeating the negative comment.

   "What is it about my sales presentation that makes you say it is difficult to follow?

These are just a few assertive communication techniques which everyone can practice in the workplace to manage communication menaces and create a more respectful environment.

Five Phrases That Can Dilute Your Message

Communicating to influence others often requires using high-impact language to effectively send your message. You may be reducing your ability to influence others by using softening phrases in your conversations, especially in meetings or presentations.

Here's what to say instead:

Avoid: "I could be wrong about this, but ..."
Instead: If you know your facts or if you are stating your opinion, then simply state it with confidence. Using a disclaimer (such as but) dilutes and negates your intent. Often people hear only the first few words you say, and you don't want those words to be "I could be wrong." Say, "The facts are ..."

Avoid: "I'm just the ..."
Instead: No matter what position you hold, claim it positively. State both what you can do and who else can help more effectively. "I'm the driver. Let me put you in touch with the warehouse supervisor who can answer that question."

Avoid: "I'm not really sure about that."
Instead: Say, "I don't know." Tell your listener that you will find an expert or confirm the information. "Let me find the answer and get back to you." If you can add a timeframe to your response, your posi-

tive influence on your listener goes up. Most people want assurance that they are speaking to the person that can best answer their question or handle their business.

Avoid: "In my opinion …"
Instead: Unless it's someone else's opinion you are referring to, just make your statement: "Further lay-offs will reduce productivity because …" or "I disagree with that decision because …" are two examples of this. Adding the word "because" immediately adds credibility and encourages agreement from others.

Avoid: "Is it okay if I ask a question?"
Instead: This useless question adds nothing to the flow of the discussion or your credibility. Ask the question or wait until you've heard enough to make sure the question is appropriate.

Try these phrases especially if you tend to have a passive communication style. Don't aim to lose every phrase; rather, shoot for more assertive statements if you find you aren't being taken seriously.

When Conversational Styles Clash

Different conversational styles can cause some of the funniest, if not costliest, misunderstandings. Interpretation of spoken messages involves more than just understanding the words. Intonation, volume, pitch, and the rate of speech must be interpreted correctly and within the framework of the speaker's style.

These conversational style differences can be traced to culture, gender, regional influences, and familial style. Fast-talking Northerners and slower-paced Southerners both send the wrong message to listeners who are unaccustomed to the idiosyncrasies of those styles. Such differences in styles are illustrated in the following story:

My sister and I were having an animated conversation regarding a business we were starting. Her boyfriend at the time, who was visiting from Scotland, was listening to our conversation from another room. The more my sister and I came up with ideas and visions for our new business, the louder and more animated we became.

At some point, my sister went into the kitchen only to find her boyfriend visibly upset. When asked what the problem was, he confessed that he was distraught because we were arguing so vociferously. He urged my sister to pack her bags as he didn't feel it was appropriate to be staying in my home if the two of us couldn't get along.

My sister burst out laughing when she realized that he had interpreted our vivacity for anger. He didn't buy this explanation at first, as his conversational background could only interpret high volume, lively pace, and an energetic pitch as inharmonious.

True enough, my sister and I had different points of view, but that evening we felt we had made tremendous headway in mapping out a mutually acceptable direction for our venture. We were actually elated that our conversation shed light on the fact that we were more in agreement than not, and we were excited to get started in our new endeavor.

You see, we had grown up in a large Italian family and had to compete with five brothers to be heard. Explosive emotions, talking over one another, and a culture that revered males meant my sister and I either had to learn how to compete or give up and hide.

This same type of misinterpretation happens frequently in the workplace. Paying close attention to the demeanor of the people you are speaking with is critical to correctly understanding the true meaning inside a conversation.

If something doesn't feel quite right, ask yourself if your interpretation is skewed by an unfamiliar conversational style.

Listen Up!

I am going to suggest that most people are poor (or at best, fair) listeners. If you don't believe you are a poor listener, then consider the list below. You might walk away with a different belief. In fact, you might wonder how anyone manages to listen without misunderstanding others, considering all the hoops we put messages through.

Incoming messages drop through several filters a before a final interpretation is created. The listening usually begins from your point of view (autobiographically) and rarely from true empathy. Listening from the speaker's standpoint takes energy, awareness, and understanding.

Consider the filters that "color" your listening and decide for yourself whether or not your skills could use a little help.

Education Level: A listener who feels intimidated by education or status might be thinking, "I'm not smart enough," or "They think they are better," and hear your message from a disadvantaged or resentful point of view. Reverse the situation and the thoughts, and you can see how much a speaker's education level affects all listeners.

Culture: Ethnicity, customs, and traditions are filters that are addressed a bit more openly, as suggested by the popularity of diversity training. Visual components that indicate or suggest a different culture may help the aware listener. He or she could use the clues as a reminder to consider how the speaker's background might support their viewpoint. Conversely, the unaware listener uses the differences to support their own opinion.

Economic Background: The "I worked for everything" listener might use this filter to avoid believing the more "economically advantaged" speaker. Like the other "message sifters" mentioned, economic background can be a barrier to empathetic listening no matter which side of the economic coin you were born on.

Family Messages: Was your family open and demonstrative, or indirect and more formal? Did you receive the message that people are generally good or generally evil? What obvious or subliminal messages did you grow up with? Consider how your viewpoint colors your listening. The challenge here is recognizing that other families may not have grown up the same way you did. Remember the first time you had dinner at a friend's house? Was the dinner conversation lively and encouraged, or were controversial topics hush-hush? Think about it.

Birth Order: I admit that, as the middle child of seven and the first female child, my mediating qualities were enhanced. Listening to someone who loves conflict and takes the contrarian viewpoint just for fun is a challenge for me. How has being the only, first, last, or middle child tinted your listening ability?

These are just five of the filters that incoming messages go through before we actually hear the message. I could have included religion, personality, and location, but the point remains the same — listening from your audience's perspective requires an acute awareness of your own filters first.

Practice attentiveness and understanding to become a better listener. Misunderstandings will decrease — and you might just learn something.

The Five Biggest Listening Mistakes that Can Hurt Your Career

Excellent listeners, regardless of their job function, brand themselves as leaders. Poor listeners can damage their careers and never know why. Don't let these five listening mistakes hurt your chance for success.

Mistake #1: Judging instead of focusing. Where do you put your focus when others are speaking to you? Are you mentally judging their clothing, appearance, speech patterns, accent, presentation, or mannerisms instead of listening to the message?

This behavior sends the message that you don't like this person and you are going to tune out the entire communication before he or she utters a word.

Instead, focus on the value of the content he or she is providing. Suspend your judgment for a short time, and you might learn something helpful or important.

Mistake #2: Making assumptions. Do you frequently finish other people's sentences? Do you use phrases such as "I know that already" before you have heard a complete sentence?

The message you send is, "I know more than you do, so let me help you out." This is not only rude behavior, but it will brand you as a "know-it-all."

Instead, listen patiently, ask clarifying questions, and paraphrase the speaker's words. Seek to understand the speaker and their message before making suppositions. This positive behavior will brand you as an excellent communicator.

Mistake #3: Correcting and disagreeing. Do you jump in to say, "The problem with that is ..." or "That won't work" before the speaker has even completed a thought? Do you constantly interrupt to set him or her straight?

At first glance, the message here is overconfidence, but really the cause is low self-esteem.

Instead, listen entirely until the speaker finishes. It is possible that you are missing a key point you hadn't considered. If you do disagree, calmly state your position. Vow to place learning over the need to be right.

Mistake #4: Impatient behavior. Are you guilty of foot-tapping, looking over your speaker's shoulder to see what else is going on, or checking your watch?

Clearly, you are sending a message that says, "My time is more important than your time." Superiority is not the behavior of a leader.

Instead, practice the basics of listening. Use eye contact, a head nod or two, and nonverbal gestures to encourage the speaker to continue. Brand yourself as a leader with superior listening skills.

Mistake #5: Reacting to a single point while ignoring the whole message. Do you find yourself responding emotionally to trigger words or phrases, dismissing the entire message before it is delivered? The message here is, "Don't waste my time; I've made up my mind."

Instead, become known as a fair person who listens with an open mind. Create a safe place for people to share information, ideas, and opinions. Learn to develop your listening skills and you will become known as a great communicator.

"Speak when you are angry and
you'll have the best speech you'll ever regret."

~ Dr. Laurence J. Peter

Difficult
Conversations

"Make 'extreme listening' your sport of choice!"

Section 3 – Salient Points

☑ Separate behavior from personality when giving negative feedback.

☑ Extreme listening is the most powerful tool you can use to open the gateway to understanding and agreement.

☑ Cooperation comes when people know and feel they are a part of something bigger.

☑ Connect your head to your heart before engaging your mouth.

☑ If you caused an uncomfortable situation for a coworker or supervisor, correct it quickly and in person.

☑ Hone your negotiation skills to increase your self-confidence and leadership abilities.

☑ Take a moment to focus on your own feelings before engaging with a workplace bully. Realize that you have control over your response.

☑ Increase the number of high-risk conversations you have each month to boost your ability to handle difficult conversations.

☑ Choose the person you find the most difficult to listen to and challenge yourself to learn something positive about him or her.

Ten Steps for Giving Negative Feedback

The challenge with giving negative feedback is getting a positive outcome that lasts. Giving opinions and advice is not for managers only. Team members often need to counsel each other in order to meet objectives. Coworkers often have to give downbeat information in an effort to obtain fairness.

Here is the ten-step formula to use when giving negative feedback:

1. **Examine your intentions.** What end result would you like to see? Focus on the outcome rather than your emotions. If you are thinking about revenge rather than results, be honest with yourself. Refrain from any discussion until you can shift from a negative to a neutral or positive frame of mind.

2. **Understand the kind of feedback you are providing.** Is it to find a solution to a disagreement? Is it to give direction? Or is it to express dissatisfaction? Asking those questions and making those distinctions helps you stay focused on the response and the behavior you are seeking.

3. **Pick the right time and place.** Tossing in your comments as an afterthought to a casual conversation is not going to yield the results you would like. Blurting out your opinions in a crowded break room and shouting over a noisy background are never appropriate, either. Pick a place that is quiet and convenient for both parties.

4. **Separate behavior from the personality.** Assume that change will happen as a result of the conversation. Visualize the outcome and use the positive energy to keep the conversation on track.

5. **Look to the future and forgive the past.** You can't undo past behavior, and dwelling on it serves no one. Use the "next time" approach to create a better atmosphere for change.

6. **Know the result you desire.** Be specific. Skirting an issue and hoping for a change is not a strategy. Be clear and communicate the outcome you are expecting.

7. **Check for understanding.** Don't assume your message has been heard and interpreted as you intended. Emotions tend to color the communication. Allow time for processing and ask for your listener's interpretation of what was heard.

8. **Ask for interpretation of the desired behavior.** Hearing the message is easy — actually comprehending, applying, and assimilating the new behavior is hard. This is the step that is most often forgotten. What you are seeking is to have the other person thinking the same way you think — no easy task. Talk about the benefits of the change, not just the features. Spend time uncovering fears and misunderstandings. Discuss roadblocks to incorporating the change into daily behavior. Allow an opportunity for application.

9. **Discuss further action.** What tools or resources might be needed to ensure that the change can be carried out? Is a schedule or mentoring or further development required?

10. **Stay involved.** Acknowledge positive actions. Notice assimilation of the new thinking and behavior. It is no surprise that workers appreciate recognition — don't be stingy with words of encouragement and thanks.

How to Handle Difficult Conversations with Empathy

Difficult conversations at work are rarely approached from the standpoint of listening rather than speaking. Yet listening with empathy is the most powerful communication tool you can use to calm people down and open the gateway to understanding and agreement.

Rather than worrying about what you are going to say, arm yourself with superb listening skills. Go beyond superficial or pretend listening and practice truly empathetic listening.

Here are five ways to listen, communicate effectively, and avoid misunderstandings:

1. **Decide to be fully present and give your complete attention to the speaker.** Relax. This is your opportunity to learn something, so you don't have to worry about what to say next.

2. **Listen for what might be going on under the surface.** This doesn't mean to judge; rather, it means to listen for feelings, attitudes, values, and fears. What point of view has the speaker taken that you might not have considered before? In what ways does that point of view make sense, even if you disagree? Open yourself up to learning something about the speaker that you might not have understood prior to the conversation. Ask yourself why he might feel this way.

3. **Difficult conversations stem from fear, regardless of any outward expression of aggression or attack.** Keeping this in mind gives you the opportunity to listen for the basis of that fear. Fear is universal, regardless of your position. Think about it — if you feel uncomfortable or apprehensive about engaging in a difficult conversation, then it is likely the other person feels the same way. What might he or she fear the most? Is it job loss, loss of respect, the perception of incompetence, reprisal, looking foolish, or the inability to clearly make a point? Simply taking on this outlook will give you a deeper understanding and the opportunity to calm down and broaden your knowledge.

4. **Practice listening to the entire message without reacting emotionally** to any single point that triggers a strong response in you. Taking things out of context causes misunderstandings and is disrespectful to the speaker. You just might be surprised to learn that you agree on more than you thought you did, once you hear and understand the whole message.

5. **Ask if there is anything more the speaker needs to express before responding.** This might be the most difficult skill to practice. After all, who wants to hear more, especially if it involves complaints, criticisms, or critiques? But this might be the most important question of all. It absolutely tells the speaker that you are willing to hear them out and that you understand that the first round of expression might be filled with emotion rather than with logic. Nothing says "I'm listening" like the question, "Is there anything else?" Someone who feels as though they are being heard for the first time will become open to the possibility that an agreement can be reached.

Embarrassing Conversations, Empathetic Solutions

D ifficult conversations come in all shapes and sizes. Handling them effectively means you will need an arsenal of clever, creative, and direct solutions. The most challenging conversations seem to be the ones involving personal habits. Handling poor performance, pointing out unacceptable behavior, or firing an employee are often easier than handling conversations about inappropriate clothing, bad breath, or body odor. These conversations tend to go one of two ways, with the possibility of embarrassment for both parties.

The first response from the offender upon notification is gratitude. Clueless to their own awareness, your conversation suddenly creates an epiphany about their effect on others. The change is made and no further conversations are required. The alternate response is denial, defense, and anger. The key is to keep a neutral and nonjudgmental but empathetic voice focused on the desired change. Refrain from downplaying or diluting the offense, as this may appear as a reprieve. Allow some venting, request the change, repeat if necessary, and name the consequence if the change does not occur.

Challenging as these conversations are with coworkers, they leap into another stratosphere when they involve customers. I managed an upscale home furnishings store in the south, where it was not uncommon for customers to shop in casual, warm-weather clothing. On one particular day, a woman came in and explained that her mother and aunt were going to stay outside and enjoy the sun while she shopped.

What she failed to explain was that her elderly and obese relatives had stripped down to bikini tops and short shorts and plopped themselves down on the curb, blocking the walkway to the entrance. I mean no disrespect to large people or the chronologically challenged, as this behavior would be just as unacceptable even for nubile teens. But the grey hair and rubbery rolls of exposed and sweat-glistened flesh created a visual assault which seemed offensive to some of our regular design clients, who voiced their displeasure at having to view and alter their path to get around the sun bunnies.

Horrified, my staff paged me and pleaded for immediate action. I must admit I was a bit stumped as to how to best approach this situation. I could invite them inside to enjoy the air conditioning; but on second thought, did I really want to showcase this spectacle sitting on a $4,000 loveseat? No — I needed to come up with another solution. My staff was now staring at me, wondering how exactly I was going to approach our sun-bathing beauties. I took a deep breath, put on a big smile, and walked towards the curb squatters, still not quite sure what was going to come out of my mouth.

"Hello, ladies. I see you're enjoying the sunshine and I wish I could join you. But I can't imagine this curb is very comfortable, so I'm going to suggest you enjoy the lovely picnic table our neighbor has put out for his customers to enjoy. Let me give you a hand getting up."

It worked like a charm and they were grateful for my extended hospitality. Lucky for us, the neighbor's location was fifty feet away on the other side of a slight ravine. Problem solved. Back inside the store, my staff, who had watched in amazement as I dislodged the offenders, begged me to tell them what I said. I told them. The lesson here is to smile, then align yourself in a relatable way ("wish I could join you"), and follow up with a solution that suits everyone.

Seven Steps to Turn Resistance into Cooperation

Employee resistance to change in the workplace is nothing new. Leaders and managers accept the pushback that comes with rolling out new procedures, changes in operations, shifts in hours or status, or even the loss of a prime parking space. How you deal with resistance makes the difference between gaining cooperation and respect and being viewed as an uninvolved, autocratic administrator.

Whether the resistance comes from a single dissenter or an entire department, use the following steps to gain cooperation:

Step 1. Clearly state what you want, when you want it, and how it will affect individual jobs. Use a firm but neutral or positive tone of voice. Refrain from conveying disappointment, anger, or defeat. Your particular situation or location will dictate the appropriate vocal expression.

Step 2. Decide beforehand how much time you will allot for objections, groaning, and griping. Inform the person or team you are addressing about the time limit. Let them vent.

Step 3. Listen in order to understand concerns. What underlying emotions are behind the complaints? What are the real fears behind the protests? Often the real fears will not be voiced in the initial session and, until further questioning, your understanding may be based on false assumptions.

Step 4. Check your perceptions by reflecting back your understanding of the concerns. Do not allow another round of protests; rather, simply check for confirmation.

Step 5. If appropriate, ask for suggestions. Not every circumstance will allow for this, but to the degree that employees feel engaged in the process, cooperation can happen more quickly. Once again, do not allow suggestions to go on forever. Keep the conversation on suggestions only — not grousing. Be involved. Listen and list possibilities without judging. Put it all down. Be open to viable proposals.

Step 6. Suggest a review or an opportunity to revisit the impact of the change after a test run or implementation. This is a good practice to put into place whenever a new procedure or shift is introduced, regardless of the initial response. Small changes made at this revisit may prevent a complete breakdown of cooperation, which can happen if the negative effects of changes are left unchecked. This is also an excellent opportunity to increase face time, engage employees, and learn something new.

Step 7. If these steps fail, explain the costs of noncooperation. Change is what makes an organization stay competitive, robust, and profitable. Dissenters may be in the wrong position or job, so act accordingly.

Cooperation comes when people know and feel they are part of something bigger. Employees know that changes occur but welcome the opportunity to influence the outcome and success. However, communicating openly and involving employees by asking for suggestions does not mean they make the final decision. Be a leader — listen, learn, and then implement.

Five Keys to Keeping Your Composure in Thorny Conversations

Nothing is more stressful than engaging in a difficult conversation, except anticipating such a conversation. Handling a thorny conversation without losing your self-control comes from practice, perspective, and awareness. With a few tips, you can conquer the fear, hold the conversation, and still walk away feeling good about yourself while not leaving the other party devastated.

Learn these five keys to handling tricky conversations and keeping cool under stress:

1. **Remember who you are.** This is a piece of advice I learned years ago, and it has helped me cope with the anxiety that comes from thinking about difficult conversations. You have the right to honor yourself as a person of integrity (if you are). You have the right to voice your opinion about an uncomfortable topic without explaining yourself. You might not change another person's opinion or behavior, but only you know who you are.

2. **Remember where you are.** The workplace is a bit like the Internet — once the words are out of your mouth, they can't be taken back. The saying "the walls have ears" suggests that conversations (no matter how confidential) have a way of becoming viral. A juicy tidbit of conversation begs to be forwarded. Choose your words carefully.

3. **Connect your head to your heart.** This was another sage comment directed at me during a particularly difficult time in my life. It seemed that my communication skills were being governed by my stress level. Everything I was saying sounded like a confrontation, disapproval, or annoyance. My head was not connecting to my heart. Connect your words to your compassion rather than raw emotion. More than likely, the anticipated communication is probably difficult for all parties involved.

4. **Rehearse your comments.** Have you ever come up with the perfect comment to a remark, only it was long after the conversation was over? You are not alone. Knowing what you want to say, how to say it, and saying it in an organized manner comes with planning, not shooting from the hip. A loose comment in the heat of the moment has a way of distorting your intention. Write out the anticipated conversation or solicit the ear of someone not emotionally involved in the situation to listen to your words and your voice. Rehearsing increases your chances of being successful at making all of your points, even if emotions threaten to take over.

5. **Consider the long-term impact.** What impact or result will occur moments after your conversation? Will the result last more than a few moments? What about the impact in a few weeks or in a year from now? You'll discover that some conversations won't need to happen at all, but don't make that an excuse for not having the ones that do. Thinking about the long term impact allows you to put things into perspective. Perspective goes a long way towards guiding the tone, words, and intention of your communication.

A small shift in your behavior could make the difference between keeping or losing a customer, between maintaining morale or creating chaos, or between motivating someone to do better or deflating their self-worth.

Correcting Communication Confusion

Workplace misunderstandings can be stressful and damaging to your career, especially if you created the communication confusion. Knowing how to handle communication blunders while keeping your composure can save a career, a reputation, or a business relationship.

Early in my career, I inadvertently created a situation where a client requested to work with me instead of the original salesperson who was working on her project. As the policy was to be helpful but not overly engaging while assisting other colleagues' clients, I had no intention of causing her to make that request. But while assisting her during the original salesperson's absence, my enthusiasm and willingness to answer her questions apparently crossed the line from helpful to fully engaged. (Please note that I don't believe this is necessarily a bad thing, but that belongs in another book.)

Knowing that I had created a situation which could cost me my relationship with a respected colleague, as well as possibly losing a client, I acted as quickly as possible. Since my coworker was working the day following my slip-up, I got up early (even though it was my day off) and went in to work to speak with her. The office grapevine had already delivered the news and she was angry and not overly receptive to my conversation.

No matter how her emotions showed, I knew I had to keep mine in check. I apologized and told her that I respected her work and our relationship. I spoke honestly and intently, and stayed with it despite her initial reluctance to acknowledge me. Eventually, she realized that I had made a special effort to correct the misunderstanding and that I valued our working relationship more than the short-term gains of making a sale.

As you might guess, correcting communication mishaps has a lot to do with values. Having good working relationships is a quality-of-life issue. Work can be challenging enough without the added stress of hostile or unfriendly coworkers on a daily basis.

If you find yourself in a similar situation, keep these tips in mind:

Apologies are always appropriate, but be mindful of your timing, framing, and mode of delivery. Don't allow emotions to be the message. Use your words to correct misunderstandings and seek confirmation that your apology was heard correctly.

If you caused an unfortunate or difficult situation for a coworker or supervisor, intentionally or not, correct it quickly and in person. This is no time to rely on e-mail or other electronic communication. Use the phone only when an in-person delivery isn't possible.

If you realize your blunder the moment your words leave your mouth, apologize immediately. Take the onus and do the right thing without adding dramatics. A heartfelt, "I apologize. That comment was uncalled for," will go a long way in mending a regrettable comment.

Negotiation — A Persuasive Conversation

Negotiations and persuasive communication skills are frequently needed by business professionals. Influential and persuasive conversations require tact, awareness, timing and the right words.

Focus on the following points:

1. **Keep control of your emotions.**
   Negotiating can trigger emotions when you fail to realize that you are an adult speaking to another adult. Too frequently people fall into the "child-to-adult" role where pleading replaces negotiating. If you find that your emotions are surfacing, excuse yourself from the situation rather than blundering ahead while blubbering.

2. **Know what you want — specifically.**
   Don't leave the details of your request up to someone else. I once negotiated the terms of my firing. I was young and caught off guard (most people are) and found myself losing control. (See #1 above.) I stated that I wanted to continue the conversation, but that I needed to leave the building for a short time. This gave me time to collect myself and make decisions about what would serve me best in the next few weeks.

Getting some air and clearing my head was the best thing I could have done. I came back and asked for:

a) an office to do a job search,
b) that the office be located in another building (I had the option available)
c) access to a receptionist who would receive and for ward my calls without comment
d) access for at least three weeks.

I don't know where I got the nerve to ask for this, but I felt that the firing was groundless. I got everything I requested. And the best part? I got a job with a 43 percent pay increase within a week. Know what you want.

3. **Know who you are talking to.**
   Will you be speaking to a dominant personality with a tendency toward angry outbursts? Or will you be lucky enough to be engaging a logical or highly empathetic person? Tailor your conversation to the way they like to communicate. Match your energy and pace to the person you are engaging. Use your body to your advantage, regardless of your actual size. I have learned to use my posture, presence, and stance to appear much larger than my five-foot height.

Negotiating is a learned skill necessary for business success. Invest some time to learn the language, and you'll begin to feel at ease in any persuasive conversation.

How to Negotiate and Get What You Want

Everybody negotiates — a good deal of daily communication is really some type of negotiation. Parents negotiate with their kids, employees negotiate with employers, and buyers negotiate with sellers.

Negotiation is a communication skill that helps you get what you want from someone while still maintaining a relationship. Without maintaining the relationship, all you have is confrontation. In business, honing your negotiation skills will not only help you grow your business, but it will increase your self-confidence and develop your leadership skills.

Here are the steps necessary to engage in powerful negotiations:

Prepare: Know specifically what you want.
- Be firm on your bottom line — that is, the least you will accept or your walk-away point.
- Know what the other party's bottom line is — or give it your best estimate.
- Develop a strategy for every possible counterpoint or objection.
- Get as much information as possible about the person (and their organization, if applicable) that you'll be dealing with.
- Learn about policies, cultures, and typical business practices if

you are negotiating with someone from another organization.
- Rehearse possible scenarios so you'll feel confident and have the proper mindset.
- Your body language will play a strong role in your ability to communicate effectively, so practice.

Preparation is the single most important step in the negotiation process. Never walk in cold to a challenging situation.

Propose: This is your opportunity to state your case.
- If you've done your homework, you should sound calm, assertive and organized.
- Believe in your request and state it without wavering. If you are asking for a raise, state your accomplishments and follow with, "I believe it's time for my compensation to catch up with my achievements." Then shut up and let the other side talk.
- Your proposal must be significantly higher than your bottom line. This allows room for compromise.
- Your objective is to get the other side to see how things look from your point of view and obtain buy-in.
- You can get what you want without agreement, but buy-in paves a path for future negotiations.

Negotiate: The opposing side will accept, dismiss, or counter your proposal.
- You make your counteroffer, and the process repeats until an agreement or a breakdown in communication occurs.
- Keep your bottom line and walk-away points in mind.
- Refrain from backing down. Remember, he who speaks first after an offer loses.
- Remaining calm and focused is essential, even if that means breaking for time-outs.

This is the dance of compromise, and if you are prepared you can enjoy the process.

Outcome: Agreement or disagreement. One way or another, you will come to a mutually accepted option — even if it is "agreeing to disagree." Always come away with your self-respect intact.

Learning to negotiate is a critical professional skill. Early in my career, I learned how to negotiate the price of piece goods with Japanese trading companies. I honed my skills, got the best prices, and had loads of fun doing it. Negotiating is a skill that has served me well. I've negotiated my hiring price, my firing price, and everything in between. You can too.

How to Deal with a Bad Boss and Keep Your Sanity

The bad, bullying, or difficult boss who manages by exploding uses fear as his or her motivating weapon. The truth is, those bosses are operating from fear — expressing their feelings instead of communicating. I don't advocate working with emotionally explosive bosses, but if you find yourself in this position, there are few strategies you can implement until you find an alternative career opportunity.

1. **Dealing with an explosive boss is similar to walking in a mine field** — there's no telling when your next step is going to be the wrong one. In extreme cases, any interaction might set off his or her fuse. Keeping this in mind, try to determine what sets off their explosive reactions most frequently. Is it lateness, errors, bad news, missed deadlines, or lost business that generates a response fueled by feelings? Understand that fear is the underlying emotion, and control what you can — your response.

2. **Take a moment to focus on your own feelings before engaging with your boss.** Are you experiencing fear before every encounter? Is your fear realistic? In other words, if you fear losing your job, is that really justified? Are you concerned about the yelling escalating into violence? Are you afraid you won't be able to control your own response? Use this moment to realize that these scenarios are unlikely and that the yell-

ing is simply "acting out," much like a toddler who can not yet express themselves. Breathe. Realize that you have control over your response.

3. **Maintain your calmness.** Difficult as that might be, the result is quite powerful. First, you'll feel better and second, your calm exterior may be the model of behavior your boss needs to experience in order to calm himself down. Allow the tantrum to play out without responding. Only 911 operators can say "calm down." When appropriate, acknowledge your boss's feelings and offer alternatives. "I can see you are upset by this, and yet I need to get a decision (or whatever you need)." Offer to continue the discussion to resolve the matter now or later.

4. **Do not become a part of the tirade.** Just as an upset customer wants to be heard, allow your boss's venting to occur. Offer alternatives. Be pleasant, firm, and steady in your response.

5. **There may be times when the above steps do not work.** If the ranting continues to escalate, it might be wise to excuse yourself from the situation. In a neutral voice you might say, "Excuse me, John, I think it would be best for me to return to my desk until we can discuss this without yelling." Again, stay calm.

Working with an explosive boss is unproductive and unhealthy. Practice this strategy until things change for the better — until your boss gets enlightened or you get a new boss.

Top Ten Tips to Improve
Your Communication at Work

If you are serious about wanting to improve your communication skills at work, then take a peek at my top ten tips and choose just one to work on today. Tomorrow, pick another and repeat the process.

10. **Choose the person you find the most difficult to listen to and challenge yourself to learn one new thing about him or her.** Be deliberate. Initiate a conversation by asking an open-ended question about this person and prepare to listen for 60 seconds without interrupting.

    I once asked a purchasing agent, who rarely got excited about anything and seemed a bit unapproachable, where he was going on vacation. I was surprised to learn that he loved to gamble in Las Vegas. His answer not only prompted more questions, but provided me with a new way to approach him in the future.

9. **Schedule a quarterly feedback conversation with your manager or supervisor.** Don't wait for your annual review. This is a critical conversation that both managers and employees rarely approach with positive anticipation, yet it is the perfect opportunity to increase your value. Ask for advice and put it to work.

8. **Increase the number of "high-risk" conversations you have**

each month. If you're interested in joining the sales team while you're currently manning the front desk, make it a point to interact with the sales manager more frequently. Ask a question that shows your interest and intelligence. "Sarah, what do the top sales people have in common that makes them successful?"

7. **Vow to eliminate one repetitive phrase, over-used cliché, or credibility-killer phrase from your conversations.** Trust me, no one is going to miss hearing you say "in these economic times."

6. **Complain only to the person who can handle your concern.** Don't go home and whine to your spouse or unload to your cubicle neighbor about the unfairness of your boss.

5. **If you are constantly in conflict with the same person, stop and ask yourself, "What is another way I could approach this person?"** Consider what fear or frustration this person may be experiencing and approach them from that point of view. Decide who you will need to be in order to make that connection: generous, open, forgiving, compassionate?

4. **Record your conversations.** Replay them when you can listen with a neutral ear. Listen closely for how frequently you interrupt, what message your voice sends, and how well you enunciate.

   In my early twenties, I taped an interview for a class project and was horrified to hear myself say "true the park" instead of "through the park." I only needed to hear it once to eliminate it from my speech forever.

3. **Curb destructive comments.** They serve no one.

2. **Eliminate "the problem with that is …" from your conversations,** or any similar phrase. Consider what is right about something before you decide it won't work.

1. **Listen. Really listen.** You'll improve your communication instantly. Listen for underlying emotions and values. Listen for the real issues. Listen for understanding. Listen to determine what your response should be rather than knowing your response beforehand. Listen to learn. Listen to be a leader.

Learning how to handle critical conversations in the workplace takes putting the willingness to learn above the need to be right.

"Because I said so."

-Any Parent

Attitude
Interviewing
Hiring
Managing
Appreciating

"An encounter with one person in the organization is an encounter with the whole organization."

Section 4 – Salient Points

☑ Become a solution-oriented person who focuses on actions that move things forward.

☑ How successful you are at communicating determines the degree to which you will be successful in business.

☑ People just want to be acknowledged and appreciated — everyone benefits.

☑ If you want to create results, clarify expectations and leave no room for assumptions.

☑ Asking the right questions is more important than answering questions with the right answers.

☑ Hire for attitude over aptitude.

☑ Help coworkers overcome communication limitations.

Have You Listened to Yourself Lately?

There are two kinds of people in the world: people who focus on solutions and people who take delight in expanding problems. You can tell the difference by listening to what they say.

Solution-oriented people rarely spend time assigning blame. They are forward-thinking and take actions that move things along. These creative problem solvers use both logic and random input to work out challenges.

Personally or professionally, solution-oriented types use language that is distinctly positive without being Pollyannaish. You'll hear them say, "What's another possibility?" or "How about this option?" They tend to be collaborative in an effort to generate ideas. Overall, they are more optimistic and enjoyable to be around.

Problem-oriented people love to stay mired in the mess. Rehashing what happened, declaring who is to blame, and adding to the predicament are their specialties. They excel at limiting possibilities for their own growth. Every option put on the table is shot down for one reason or another. They offer no solutions and are focused only on the past.

You'll hear them say, "I knew this wouldn't work!" or "I can't do that!" These problem-focused types tend to be complainers and small thinkers. Being around them is enervating and distressing.

I can't imagine living inside the head of a problem-expander. Every obstacle is approached as insurmountable. These are the people I just want to shake and say, "Have you listened to yourself lately? Can you hear how negative you sound?"

Experience has shown that problem-expanders are remarkably unaware of how they sound to others. To be fair, they do pay attention to perceived injustices, senseless systems, and problems that others ignore, and there is a need for that kind of scrutiny in today's world where even egregious violations are overlooked.

However, if you sound like a naysayer, now is the time to stop pointing out issues and start offering constructive resolutions.

Have you listened to yourself lately?

Expressing Yourself for Business Success

How successful you are at communicating determines the degree to which you will be successful in business. Writing, listening, connecting, and selling all require effective communication skills. Where do you stand?

"The way we communicate with others and with ourselves ultimately determines the quality of our lives."

Tony Robbins said that, and he was right. The good news is that communication skills can always be improved. Start by evaluating your current ability.

Here are six ways to determine how successful you are at expressing yourself:

Do you ask for and listen to feedback? Most people are fearful of doing this. Few people like to hear the unvarnished truth about how well they come across to others. Yet this may be the key to unlocking your business growth. Ask people you trust to give you an honest response. Ask a mix of family, friends, and business associates to get a better profile. Then listen — really listen. Decide what might be true and choose to make some changes. Be open to the information and thank them for their honesty.

What kind of clients do you have? Are you working with people you enjoy and respect? Do they express themselves well? Do they recommend you to others?

Would you want to associate with you? What message do you send to others about the people you socialize and do business with? Do you have a variety of associations? "You can't fly with eagles if you're hanging out with turkeys" is a saying that holds a lot of truth. Take a critical look at your relationships and ask yourself if you need to make some changes.

How careful are you about your written or viral communications? Have you become lazy about grammar and spelling? Do you speak or write in "text"? Do your articles, reports, or books have numerous errors that erode your credibility?

How well do you follow up? This is a big one. Success in personal and business relationships has everything to do with how well you follow up. This includes the courtesy of responding to an RSVP on an invitation. Failure to respond affects business — it doesn't matter if it's a wedding or a business function — the consequence is far-reaching. If this were the benchmark for successful communication, most people would be in trouble. On the business side, customer dissatisfaction is overwhelmingly strong concerning the lack of follow-up.

How did you do?

Appreciation — The Key to Morale-Building

"The deepest craving of human nature is the need to be appreciated."
~ William James

Managers and leaders often find that even the most cooperative teams occasionally fall into a morale funk. If job-cutting rumors, slow sales, and the constant reminder from the media of a troubled economy make it difficult to keep your team upbeat and positive, try this exercise.

This activity will shift your team's thinking and outlook. It promotes goodwill and a deeper level of appreciation among team members. You'll be amazed at how quickly it works.

Step 1: Write down one good thing about each team member. Ask yourself why you are grateful that he or she is a part of your department, unit, or area of responsibility.

Be positive, original, and honest. Write a note that reflects each person's nature and refrain from generic comments. Even the most annoying or least productive person has one redeeming quality, even if it is to force you to be more patient.

Print and cut each "appreciation note" into fortune-cookie size.

Step 2: Call your team together and read your notes aloud to the group. Then have them write their own notes for each of their coworkers. Set the ground rules: positive comments only, no back-handed compliments, and everyone must get a note.

Again, encourage creative and truthful comments. If someone is having difficulties writing about a coworker, encourage a bit of humor. Light-hearted notes such as "John, I'm so grateful you fill the candy bowl daily'" is acceptable, but "John, I'm so grateful you sit on the other side of the office'" is not. Again, use the fortune-cookie size.

If team members are new or have not had the opportunity to get to know each other well, instruct them to write what they sense about the other person. New team members will bring a fresh, untainted eye to their compliments.

Step 3: Ask for volunteers to read their notes but don't force it, especially if the group is large. Have team members exchange their notes and give coworkers time to read and acknowledge each other. People will want to read their "good fortunes" over and over.

The best part — everyone smiles. Five, ten, or fifteen hand-written fortune notes appreciating and affirming a person's value and worth goes so much further than a party, a seminar, or a verbal thank-you ever will.

This exercise works immediately and the results will linger for some time. Coworkers and clients will profit from the shift in attitude and morale. You'll notice the notes posted around where they can be read daily by the recipient. Most people just want to be acknowledged and appreciated. Everyone benefits.

You Can't Get There If You Don't Know Where You're Going

A common complaint from managers revolves around unmet expectations from direct reports and their teams. Similarly, workers complain that expectations are not clear and leave too much room for misunderstandings and assumptions.

Let's look at some root problems and solutions.

Problem: Failure to clarify the desired results or assuming the outcome is understood.

Management is often working within a larger framework with information that has not been made available to their direct reports. Think of this information as the missing pieces that complete the puzzle picture. The manager's expected result is to reproduce the picture with all the parts as he sees it. Misunderstandings arise when the picture in the manager's head does not match the picture they have painted for their direct reports.

Solution:

1. Clarify the expectations. Paint a picture in as many ways as possible — visually, verbally, and vocally. Give a comparison to a known entity, if possible. "It should look like X with this adjustment."
2. Clearly state the required details — the non-negotiable conditions.
3. Confirm interpretation and actions.

113

Ask what was heard. Ask what that means. Ask what actions will be taken. Allow creativity and leeway to do the job as long as the end result is the same.

Problem: Systems and tools don't function as needed and departments don't work together.
Solution:
1. Provide the needed tools to do the job — including software, hardware, personnel, filing systems, proper forms, paper, etc. It is difficult to hammer nails without the nails.
2. Smooth the path between departments to eliminate the "I can't start my part until I receive this information from …" syndrome. Catch issues before they start. Ensure that all departments are coordinated with the same expected outcome.
3. Grant the authority to do the job. Often an issue between departments occurs when one department is expected to perform but has no authority to make decisions that directly affect their ability to do so. Design is often driven by manufacturing, which is driven by operating goals. If operating goals are best met by producing out-of-date products, then design can not create what the market is asking for and sales people can't meet their goals. Don't expect a quick fix. All departments need to understand their role in profitability and growth.

Problem: Deadlines are not clear and timelines with check-in points are not established.
Solution:
1. Create a project timeline which all departments agree on.
2. Create checkpoints to ensure that the project is on track for completion. Waiting and hoping it all works out in the end is a perfect strategy for failure.

Problem: Information is not readily available, up-to-date, or accessible to achieve the expected outcome.
Solution:
1. Ensure that information and access to needed information is

in place. Sign waivers, authorizations, or requisitions beforehand. Be available or assign an alternate person to override electronic authorizations. Remove barriers that impede progress.

2. Be readily available to answer questions during execution of the project.

As a teenager, I was told by my father not to come home late. It seemed that my idea of late and his idea of late were different because no matter what time I came home — I was late! When I finally asked him what time he expected me home, he refused to name an hour. I never met his expectation because he assumed I would know what late meant. Unfortunately, this was typical of his communication style. I solved it by leaving home at an early age.

Don't make leaving the option of choice for your team. Be clear, confirm understanding, and make the outcome possible.

Six Ways to Clearly Communicate Job Responsibilities and Avoid Misunderstandings

Misunderstanding a job role causes more issues than simply unplanned downtime. Customer complaints, lost business, public safety, and legal issues are all at stake. Clear communication takes more than a paragraph in a handbook or a few sentences uttered by a human resources manager. Ideally, communicating the job description should occur not only during the interview and orientation, but also throughout the first ninety days.

Here are six ways to clearly communicate job responsibilities and decrease misunderstandings:

1. **Verbally describe the role** including tasks and expectations. The challenge here is to be both specific and broad. Use stories and examples to help create a picture that words alone fail to illustrate. Communicate the desired outcome graphically.

2. **Written job descriptions are critical** for compliance. Don't rely on an initialed checklist indicating that the new hire has read and understood the information. Written communication alone does not address questions adequately and leaves the new hire without an appropriate venue for voicing questions or concerns. Take the time to review and expand the job description using real examples.

3. **Use a detailed description** of a typical day or various scenarios the new hire might encounter. Again, using a story format helps put the new hire into the picture.

4. **Describe situations outside the job description** that the new hire would be expected to handle. Give end-result expectations and examples.

5. **After giving a verbal and written description,** ask for feedback in the form of a summary — not a list or a recitation, but a description of how they see the function and their role in making it happen. Ask how they would handle a situation and encourage details about the end results. Listen for any disconnects between their idea of the job and the actual expectations of the job. What is not being said is more important than what is being said.

6. **Ask what he or she considers their biggest challenge** in the position. Ask for a strategy for achieving results. Do not let "Hopefully, I can …" be an acceptable answer. Hope is not a strategy. Too frequently, new hires are skilled at giving the appropriate answers but have no intentions or aptitude for actually doing the function. Ask what they love best about their current job.

Clearly communicating policies, job functions, and expectations is a part of your job if you hire or manage people. Spend more time on this critical message up front and enjoy fewer misunderstandings in the future.

Five Questions You Must Ask in a Job Interview

Asking the right questions is as important as answering questions with the right answers. When you are a prospective employee, interviews are the ultimate test of your communication skills at work, so be prepared.

Take the time to compose questions that showcase your interest in the job and the organization. Questions can also be phrased to highlight your skills and talents when the interviewer hasn't given you that opportunity.

Here are five critical questions you must ask in an interview:

1. Ask for a description of a typical day on the job.

Even if the interviewer has described a typical day, ask for further details that expand on the scope of job responsibilities and functions. Often, typical day descriptions are just that — a narrow view. Ask for a bigger view with examples of tasks or additional roles you might be expected to play, such as covering for coworkers during breaks or required attendance and participation at company or charity events. Listen for responsibilities that might not be considered routine for the job you are applying for.

2 **Ask about any financial concerns you have about the organization.**

If rumors are circulating in the industry about financial difficulties, this is the time to address them. Asking a direct question in a neutral tone gives the organization the opportunity to refute rumors or explain negative news stories. It also puts them on alert should anything happen. If you take the job and the rumors turn out to be true, you'll be glad you asked.

I once took a position after the chief financial officer assured me that the company was fiscally sound despite rumors. My questions were quite direct, so when the company filed Chapter 11 bankruptcy less than three months after I took the job, I was given severance pay equal to three months of my salary. In addition, I was given access to the search firm that connected me with the now defunct business, and once again they found me a new position that started the day following the closing. Be smart — ask.

3. **Ask what behaviors your immediate supervisor considers unacceptable.**

You'll want to know what drives them crazy and what would cause immediate dismissal. This type of question indicates values. You might think that being a few minutes late is no big deal, but if your future boss expects you to be working at your desk at start time or earlier, you'll be clashing in no time. Adjust your expectations to match those of your supervisor or find another place to work.

4. **Always ask permission to take notes while the interviewer is talking.**

This single question might make the difference between receiving an offer and receiving a thanks-but-no-thanks letter.

Asking permission is not only respectful, but it indicates that you don't want to miss a single thing that is being said.

I snagged a job once simply by asking permission to take notes. I watched the interviewer's face change and knew he had made a decision to hire me in that moment. I got the sense that people rarely, if ever, asked that question even though he had asked for my permission to take notes while I was speaking. It's a simple but effective question, so ask permission and then take notes.

5. **Ask what qualities the most successful employee has and what qualities the least successful employee is lacking.**

Pay attention. If the answer to the first part of that question is perseverance or drive, then ask how that is displayed. If the lacking quality is commitment, ask what commitment looks like for them. Your objective is to match expectations with reality prior to accepting a position.

These are just five overlooked questions that candidates fail to ask. If you ask these, along with the more common questions about promotions and educational opportunities, you will make a good lasting impression and you might edge out other candidates for the job.

Listen closely and between the lines. Practice your questions as well as your answers if you want to ace an interview.

Hire for Attitude Over Aptitude

At some point in your career, you may be responsible for hiring. On-site, off-site, virtual, or reality — hire first for attitude and interpersonal skills. Tasks, skills, systems, and procedures can be taught, but a happy and positive disposition can not.

The first person a customer, potential customer, or guest has contact with sets the first impression for your entire organization, no matter how large or small. Do not underestimate the power of this first impression. Business and relationships are lost and broken during this short window of opportunity. Worse, you'll never know when a breakdown is occurring. And you'll never have the opportunity to save it.

Consider these suggestions before you begin interviewing:

- In addition to a list of skills and qualifications, have a very clear idea about your organization's culture, philosophy, and atmosphere. This may be something that solopreneurs had not considered when they first started their venture. Take some time to consider your vision for the internal and external philosophy you want your business to be known for. Even if you are only hiring an off-site virtual assistant (VA) to handle bookkeeping and electronic organization, don't neglect your future growth and an expansion of duties for your VA that might include customer contact.

- Start with your first impression. How professional, friendly, and approachable was the candidate? Did you immediately get a sense of whether or not they would fit your culture?

- Ask for stories that illustrate a candidate's ability to handle questions, queries, and complaints. Ask about the worst customer situation they have ever encountered and how they handled it. You're looking for a positive outcome.

- Using a likely scenario for your business, play the part of the customer and have your candidate role-play with you to see how they might handle a situation. Make it challenging — you are looking for the person who acts more than just appropriately on your behalf.

- If you already have staff, set up mini-interviews or casual encounters with them.

- Interview off-site, in an atmosphere more formal or more relaxed than your business culture, to gauge their comfort level and ability to interact with people of all kinds.

- If you have two equally qualified candidates, always go for the best attitude.

Attitude wins in the end. You are probably more driven than those you hire, so don't hire for a personality match to you. Hire for customer compatibility, self-esteem, and a great attitude.

Communicate by Style — The Key to Getting More Done with Fewer Do-Overs

More productivity with less misunderstanding is a universal challenge in the workplace. Learning to communicate with all communication styles is the key to fostering cooperation, respect, and understanding. Imagine how much more you could get done if everyone just got along!

Don't get me wrong — I'm not suggesting agreement at every turn. Healthy conflict produces ideas and solutions that would not likely be generated without divergent thoughts.

What I am referring to is the enormous waste of time and energy spent correcting the miscommunications that occur on a routine basis. Misinterpretations can be avoided with a keen understanding of the four basic communication styles: I call them the Governor, the Methodical, the Agreeable and the Expansive. You may know them by other titles. The concept isn't new, but it's easy to forget in daily conversations.

- **Respect the theme or driving principle for each style.**
  Governors want to do things their way and with acceleration. Methodicals focus on accuracy at all costs. Agreeables prefer consensus before taking action. Expansives favor fun while getting things done.

- **Shift your style of communicating to meet theirs if you want to be heard.**

A momentary shift in pace, eye contact, and enthusiasm level goes a long way in making a connection. For Governors, square up your body, move with a determined step, and speak quickly. With Methodicals, shift down a bit, and control emotions and body language. Agreeables like eye contact and an easy going, amiable approach. Expansives will listen if you're positive, spontaneous, and energized.

- **To request action, provide or gather information,** and avoid misunderstandings, communicate according to each style's preferred approach to work. Governors want the bottom line, so avoid wordiness and explanations. If they are not in charge, give them something to be in charge of. Methodicals want the entire explanation of the process. Spare no detail and be logical in your justification. The written word goes a long way with this thinking style. Agreeables will work hard, gather a cooperating team, and produce quality results if you remain flexible and establish a relationship first. Taking a personal interest in their feelings creates trust and collaboration. Approach Expansives with a fun attitude. Refrain from detailed explanations, and you'll get the results you seek.

- **Finally, help each style of thinker overcome their limitations.** The risk-taking Governor may miss critical details due to impatience. Pointing out essential elements will assist Governors from making faulty decisions and charging ahead towards the wrong goal. Help Methodicals by mutually deciding to use checkpoints and deadlines. Agreeables work best when their team is in accord. Speak to coworkers first, if possible. Or, let Agreeables know that it is okay to move ahead even if everyone isn't in agreement. Help Expansives keep their environment from becoming a distraction. Support their ideas while keeping them focused on the rewards of reaching goals.

Listening and communicating by style type saves time, prevents misunderstandings, and cultivates a cooperative workplace.

"If you smile at me,
I will understand because that is something
everybody, everywhere,
does in the same language."

~ Crosby, Stills and Nash

Service
Sales

"The secret to remembering names is to tell yourself you're good at it."

Section 5 – Salient Points

☑ Business etiquette plus positive personality equals excellent customer service.

☑ Would you do business with you? Spend time being your customer, evaluating everything from reputation to referrals.

☑ Essential ABCs — Articulate, Build Rapport, and Confidence.

☑ Make listening easy for your customers and coworkers — eliminate communication barriers.

☑ Smile more frequently — especially when you are on the phone.

☑ Connect with customers and coworkers by matching pace, posture, energy, and eye contact.

☑ Engage people with stories, but avoid story-telling past the "sold" signals.

☑ No matter what you are selling — ask for the sale.

Policy Plus Personality
Equals Service Success

C onsider customer service as business etiquette plus personality, If you do, you will have happy, loyal customers. Policy alone never serves customers, as it does nothing to foster business relationships.

Service is what customers expect based on your branding. Personal encounters with anyone in your company, your public image and reputation, hearsay, and web presence all contribute to your branding. Yet it is more than that. What customers believe is the only reality you need to embrace.

Business etiquette is making others feel comfortable in a business setting, not a social setting. The key to creating a great outcome for both parties often lies in the personality of the customer care representative. A rep that can only follow a script almost always infuriates customers. Hiring the best personalities and then allowing and encouraging these reps to express themselves is the opportunity to create a connection.

Look at etiquette as the framework around policy and service. Making others feel heard, comfortable, and respected is sound business advice. Yet it isn't always easy to do, especially if you are still operating in the era of the "golden rule." The "do unto others as you would have done unto you" only works if those others think and feel the same way that you do.

If you have come this far in life, you have learned the harsh reality that others don't think the same way as you do. Here's where personality and a bit of savvy can add integrity to customer service.

Policy plus politeness are good things to have in place, but they don't create, save, or enhance a customer relationship. Only personality can do that.

Some will quibble over the term "personality," but if you listen to stories about outstanding service, rarely are guidelines mentioned. No — it's the attitude, humor, empathy, and good judgment demonstrated by the interpreter of the guidelines that makes the difference. Character creates the rapport. And this is no more important than with an upset customer.

I have seen even the most out-of-control customers calmed and turned around by service providers with exceptional personalities. One front desk associate comes to mind. Her ability to sincerely, sweetly — and in the most soothing voice you ever heard — take an outraged client who was threatening to cancel an order and turn them into a fan. She knew how to listen beyond the words to personalize her conversations.

Policy, politeness, and a winning personality are the keys to outstanding customer service.

Would You Do Business with You?

S tepping into the shoes of your customer trumps everything you have ever read or been taught about what your customers want. If you have never been on the receiving side of your service, now is the time to do so.

The best players in hospitality regularly have their associates spend a night in the best and the least desirable rooms. What are they looking for? Everything.

Beyond room cleanliness, associates are asked to evaluate the experience. How comfortable is the bed? Were you able to control the temperature easily? Were extra pillows and blankets within easy reach? Was a wake-up call prompt? Were there enough hangers? Would you take a bath in the tub?

Evaluations need to go deep; otherwise, your customer will never tell you — they just won't come back.

- Spend a day being your customer. Would you do business with you? Ask yourself these types of questions as they pertain to your product or service.

- How did my first encounter with (the product or service) make me feel? Was I uplifted or frustrated?

- If you received the product in the mail, ask yourself: How prompt was the delivery? How did the packaging hold up?

What feeling did I have when I opened the product? Was it easy to use? What were my feelings after using the product? How do I now feel about the company? Note your responses.

- If you are purchasing a service, ask yourself these questions: What was my first impression? What lingering thoughts or nagging feelings do I have about the service? Was the communication open, accessible, uplifting? Am I feeling neutral, uncertain, or encouraged about the service and future encounters? Rank your answers on a 1–10 scale and note your feelings.

- Was the product or service intuitive — did it answer questions before I had them? Did it supply answers to questions I would have failed to ask but would have needed to know?

As you can see, most of these questions address your feelings about the experience. That's all that counts if you are serious about service. People buy with their emotions and justify with their own logic. No one wants to admit making a poor purchase. Yes, good products with lousy service still sell, but in challenging economic times, good service gives you the edge.

Experience your product or service as though it were your first experience with it. Now ask yourself: "What do I need to know that I wouldn't know to ask about?" This question, if answered by your product or service, can help you keep a customer and not just get one.

Put a plan in place to experience your product or service regularly. Make it comprehensive — the above examples are just a starting point. Make it mandatory for everyone, not just key people.

Become a service leader, not just a provider, and you'll be rewarded with loyal customers who love to refer you.

Do You Know Your ABCs?

Business communication practices are guidelines that most organizations have in place even if they aren't written down. Workplace communication benchmarks may include answering the phone by the second ring, sending a thank-you note, or simply being competent and courteous when answering the phone.

When business is booming, these practices tend to slide a bit. After all, who is checking to see if every customer received a follow-up call when the next customer is waiting for service?

However, in a challenging business climate, these very fundamental practices can spell the difference between survival and demise. Even savvy ball club managers have their teams "get back to basics" when they're faltering.

Do a review of these fundamental but often overlooked workplace communication practices to see if you need to get back to basics:

A – Articulation. It is so common today to hear sloppy enunciation that we begin to hear it as normal. But your customers may pay more attention to careless communication skills, especially during phone conversations. They may voice their disapproval simply by not purchasing your product or service. Poor communication skills can hurt your branding.

Help your team brush up with a few tongue twisters or engaging them in word games each week to keep skills sharp. Have fun. But don't let this elementary communication skill cost you business.

B – Build Rapport. Every customer encounter is an opportunity to build rapport. A smile, a handshake, and a name remembered are the basics. A birthday or a pet's name remembered, or a call just to ask if they have any questions should also be a part of your communication fundamentals.

Hire happy people and teach them the skills of the job. An unhappy person infects everyone with the cranky bug — don't tolerate it. There are enough enthusiastic and competent people in the market today that replacing them should be easy.

C – Confidence. A strong, confident voice sends a positive message to your customers. Customers want to feel certain that they are buying the right product or service, and a self-assured, confident but not arrogant voice can foster that feeling.

If you're not already making periodic calls to your company to hear how the phone is answered, start immediately.

Smart companies are ramping up their selling and communication skills during this challenging market. The emphasis on developing a relationship during even the shortest transaction is the new standard, no matter the size of the organization.

Take the time to hone the essential ABCs of communications before adding advanced skills. Now is not the time to let things slide. Add training and assessments, and you'll be ready when business is booming again.

Make Listening Easy for Your Customers

Communicating with your customer begins before any conversation starts. Make it easier for your customers to understand you and give them time to process information. You can decrease misunderstandings between you and your customers — as well as save time, money, and headaches — with good customer service skills.

Here are five questions you should consider when communicating with your customers:

1. Is your native language different than your customer's? Acknowledge it up front and take it on as your challenge — not theirs. Be lighthearted about the difference and encourage your customer to stop and ask for clarification at anytime. Speak at a moderate rate and stop periodically to check for understanding.

2. Are you giving a long or complicated set of instructions? Have a written set of instructions for your customer along with your verbal explanation. Use both verbal and visual communications. Don't assume that the instructions will be read and forego the verbal instructions. (Wouldn't it be great if doctors did this?) After giving long or complex instructions, acknowledge that fact and be sure to ask specific questions. Asking, "What questions do you have about the initial set-up?" allows your client a second chance to review and process the infor-

mation. Then review the next section and, again, ask what questions they might have. Keep quiet and listen for anything they might be hesitant to ask. Refrain from asking, "Are there any questions?" This is too broad and often prompts the knee-jerk "no" response. Prompt them and make it easy.

3. Are you clear about your customer's major concern? Never assume you know why a customer is choosing your services. What seems obvious to you may not be of concern to your customer. Always ask what the most important concern or challenge is before offering a solution. This is prime time to gather as much information as possible.

4. Do you fail to give basic information, assuming a customer already knows? Always repeat basic information, especially when handling a complicated purchase. Never assume your customer knows it or understands it, even if they are a repeat customer. Even a reminder can trigger a new thought or question from your customer. You might say, "As you know, we offer a several finance options ..." However, avoid cashier parrot talk. It just annoys customers.

5. Are you communicating in the way your customer hears? Pay attention to the words your customer uses and how direct they are with you. Shift your response to they way they like to receive information. If they are direct and assertive, respond in kind.

These are just a few ways you can be of service to your customer. This is the moment to create a loyal customer who enjoys doing business with you.

Five Tips for Communicating by Phone and Sending a Professional Impression

As workers and workplaces become more relaxed in appearance and protocol, it is becoming more difficult to leave a professional impression — in person or on the phone. Because the visual and nonverbal components of communication are absent when communicating by phone, it is more challenging to send a positive impression.

Consider these five tools for communicating more effectively by phone:

1. **Address the listener by name.** Use the listener's name more frequently than you would in face-to-face conversations. Everyone likes to hear their name, and this conveys to the listener that you are fully present in the conversation. Perceptions are inflated without the aid of visual communication, so addressing your listener by name sends a favorable impression.

2. **Speak at a moderately fast rate.** Counter your rate of speaking with your listener as you begin your conversation and then bring it up just a notch. Speaking too quickly may result in the impression that you are rushing to get off the phone. Conversely, speaking too slowly can make you sound less credible or cause your listener to lose interest.

3. **Use volume effectively.** Fortunately, most phones have

volume control, but why make it difficult for your listener? Matching volume with your listener is one less barrier to communication. The more considerate you are of your listener, the more professional you'll sound.

4. **Articulate and avoid annoying speech patterns.** Sloppy speaking, lingo, casual conversational patterns, or repetitive phrases may send the message that you are casual about your business dealings as well. Pronunciation and enunciation are amplified over the phone. Ahs and ums make you sound less prepared or unsure. Repetitive phrases such as "you know" or lingo used with friends or family should be avoided. "Dude" and "girlfriend" need to be left at home. Take time to listen to your speech patterns and clean up your act.

5. **Smile.** Smart sales professionals know that smiling can be heard over the phone — so can positive body language and gestures. Stand while speaking, expand your lungs, and speak with gestures, and your listener will hear the difference.

The vocal and verbal message you communicate on the phone need to match your nonverbal message, even if it can't be seen. The best way to improve your skill is to tape yourself and notice what might distract your listener or send a less than favorable impression.

A relaxed appearance tends to create a relaxed posture. Use a good chair or, better, stand up when communicating by phone. Manage your impression on the phone and you'll be regarded as credible and professional.

Five Ways to Connect with Customers to Promote and Sell More

I n today's workplace, more employees at every level are expected to promote and sell products and services. Front-line employees can enhance their communication and selling skills by learning how to connect with different behavior styles. The concept of treating others in the way they want to be treated is a powerful communication technique practiced by few.

Nonsales positions can still learn how to use behavior styles to connect with customers even within a short window of opportunity.

Here are five ways you can communicate by style type to connect with customers to promote and sell more:

1. **Use your observation skills** to gather information before you verbally engage a customer. The pace of his or her walk, posture, energy, and eye contact can provide clues as to how adjust your approach. If you are generally enthusiastic and upbeat but your customer appears to have a lower energy level than you do, drop your level a bit without losing your appeal. Try containing gestures and lowering your volume while still maintaining a genuine smile.

2. **Notice the rate, tone, and pitch of their speech.** If you encounter a direct, fast-paced booming voice, refrain from backing away. Instead be direct back while increasing your volume

appropriately. Your customer will respect your approach. If your customer is more reticent, then slow your rate of speech and drop your voice a bit.

3. **If eye contact is fleeting** or minimal and body language is aloof, you may be encountering someone that prefers less emotion and more process. If this is the case, then be sure to explain what is going to happen in the encounter step by step. If eye contact is warm and engaging, you will want to match their style.

4. **Know what is important to your customer.** Again, observation will give you some clues. Friendly, upbeat people who are quick to engage you may be less concerned about details and focused more on what your product or service can do to enhance their visibility or stature. If you're promoting a new home-delivery dry cleaning service, stress the importance of looking perfect on a moment's notice. On the other hand, if you are promoting that same service to the person whose priority is creating and maintaining relationships, then emphasize the time-saving as a means to spend more time with family.

5. **Determine how they make decisions.** This is particularly important in a short transaction. Direct, upbeat people will agree spontaneously. Direct but results-focused customers like to make quick decisions. If your customer needs to establish a relationship first, then their decision-making process will be slower while he or she ponders the impact on others. Finally, the indirect but process-oriented person will deliberate at length before coming to an agreement.

Practice these skills and make a goal of observing behaviors with each customer encounter. Slightly shift your own behavior, and your ability to communicate, connect, and sell will increase instantly.

Take Your Smile to the Market

All communication is a form of marketing or selling, but you probably don't think of it as a marketing tool. By sharpening your interpersonal skills, you can increase the perceived value of your products and services.

Here are a few tips you can use to hone your soft skills for solid results:

1. **Smile more frequently.** You might think this is silly, but the truth is that smiling changes everything. If you are working long hours, trying to overcome challenges and dealing with frustrations, you probably aren't smiling much.

   If you answer the phone or, worse, greet a customer in person while you're managing the business of business, it's unlikely that you will greet them with a smile. If you do remember to smile, I'm betting it won't be genuine. This is unacceptable. You have a business because of those customers. Treat them with respect. Smile.

   Smiling sends a powerful message about you and your business. A stress-free, heartfelt smile invites clients or prospective customers to relax and trust you. That's a potent marketing tool. Don't forget to smile when answering the phone. The tone and pitch of your voice will be more inviting — and people can tell if you're smiling or not.

The best salespeople keep a small mirror by their phones to remind them to smile when they make or answer a call. Another tip is to post a note that says "smile — you're making money" by your phone.

2. **Clean up your language.** This isn't a reminder to lose the four-letter words from your conversations (that should go without saying). It is a reminder to listen for sloppy sentence structure, garbled grammar, mumbling, jargon, and even the ten-dollar words in your speech. You don't hear yourself as others do, so record a few phone calls and casual conversations to see how you really sound to others. After listening to the play back, ask yourself if you would do business with you.

   If printed marketing materials send one message but your verbal communication sends another, that's a congruency problem. Clean it up!

3. **Ask more questions.** Listen more than you talk. Your customers will tell you everything you need to know about what to market and what products they need. You're in business to solve their problems, so make sure you know what their problems are. Don't assume you know. Ask questions. Do surveys. Invite suggestions. Don't market a product you're in love with but doesn't serve the needs of your customer. Pay attention and ask clarifying questions. Your business depends on it.

These three essential communication skills don't take a lot of time or money, but they can increase your value to your market. Smile.

Are You Guilty of This Sales-Killer?

S torytelling is an excellent communication and selling skill. But your story could replace your service if you aren't a skilled observer.

Eagerly engaging customers with stories and benefits is a good thing. Where it goes astray is when the story continues beyond the "sold" sign and you never request action. You have probably been party to a conversation like this yourself. The salesperson is so involved in their storytelling that they neglect to observe when you are sold. By the time their anecdote is finished — well, so are you and it isn't always a positive ending. Usually you're trying to escape from the well-intentioned but long-winded storyteller.

Don't let this happen to you. Enthusiasm is wonderful, but awareness and assertiveness are critical to completing a sale. Without them, you are in danger of "walking your customer out the door" or talking them out of buying. Don't laugh — it happens all the time.

Observation means being aware of the shift that takes place once a customer decides to buy. Assertiveness means asking for the sale and/or telling them what to do next.

The ready-to-buy signs can be subtle, so practice listening and observing — even on the phone! Look and listen for a shift in energy, a change in posture, or a series of questions that signals "you sold me."

The moment you see it, stop selling or storytelling and start directing instead. It might sound like this:

- Are you ready to get started?
- Would you like me to write that up for you?
- Any other questions before we put this on order for you?
- This product is offered as CD or as an MP3 file — which would you prefer?

These transaction-completing sentences should roll off your tongue. If they don't — start practicing.

The Number One Question
Sales People Fail to Ask

There's one vital sales communication skill that, if used consistently, will increase your business. Ask for the sale. In a selling situation, potential customers desire two things: solutions to problems and the assurance that they are making the right buying decision. Yet if you provided the solution, created a connection, and quelled any doubts, your customer may still walk away without further action. Why? Because you have failed to ask for their business.

Most people prefer to be guided through a sale. They want to know what action to take and when to take it. And most customers will never reveal that truth to you.

Never be afraid to ask for the sale or tell prospective customers what step to take next. Say, "Would you like to put that on order today?" or "The next step is to confirm measurements and write up the order." Even though the desired result (sale or action) may take place without this prompt, get into the habit of asking your customers for their business during every selling conversation. It eliminates the uh-oh questions: "What could the results have been?" "How many items could I have sold?" "Will they come back?"

We're more likely to take action when clearly directed to take the next step. Dubious? When was the last time an online sales page prompted you to "just type in your name and e-mail address below and click the buy now button"? I'm betting this happened to you fairly recently. These simple instructions leave no question about what to do next. Indirect communication leaves doubt and confusion. And it's true — a confused mind always says no.

If you want to save time and make more money, then practice telling people what to do. Asking closed-ended questions can accomplish the same result. "Do you prefer to take it with you or have it shipped?" is a good example. Communicate with brief, clear, and direct language. Beating around the bush or issuing confusing instructions and lengthy explanations will fail to give you the desired result. And you will fail your customer as well.

For those of you thinking this sounds harsh, abrupt, or pushy, I am not advocating hard sales tactics — just clear communication after you've established a relationship and trust and provided the proper solution for them. Asking "Would you like to have this item delivered next week?" can be said in a soft but assertive voice.

Ask for the sale — you fail to serve others if you don't.

About Allie Casey

Some people are natural-born speakers and easily win over others by knowing exactly what to say. Other people struggle with finding the right words, keeping emotions in check, and getting people to listen. The problem is that, in the workplace, everyone needs to communicate well in order to create business relationships, connect with co-workers, listen to feedback, foster teamwork, and produce timely results.

What Allie Casey does is help workers — front-line employees, direct reports, managers, CEOs, and everyone in between — to communicate more effectively, to listen with more empathy, and to decrease costly misunderstandings; in other words, to communicate with fewer headaches and better outcomes.

Allie does this through speaking, training, and coaching with a process she calls "The Invitation for Communication" — a five-step formula that will have your organization, team, or key employees communicating more effectively in no time.

Growing up in suburban New York, Allie struggled with what to say and when to say it. Mostly she said nothing — especially in school. She knew things had to change when a teacher said to her on her last day of high school, "You have been in my class for a year and I don't know what your voice sounds like." Allie knew she had to do more than listen — she had to speak. Today, Allie changes lives by helping others become powerful, effective communicators.

Allie lives in Orlando, Florida. To learn more or book Allie for your event, visit www.AllieCasey.com or call 407-313-4967.

How to Receive Your FREE Bonus Gifts

To receive your 3 FREE Bonus Downloads from *Misunderstood! The Fast Guide to Communicating at Work—What to Say, How to Say It and When to Shut Up* go to:

www.TheFastGuideToCommunicatingAtWork.com

BONUS #1 –
AN INSTANT PDF DOWNLOAD OF THE ENTIRE BOOK!
All the tips and techniques at your fingertips! Not sure how to tell your loud co-worker to pipe down—pull up the answer instantly!

BONUS #2 –
AN AUDIO DOWNLOAD OF ALL THE MAIN POINTS!
Five pages of the "BEST-OF-THE-BEST" highlights from every chapter in an audio format—listen when it's convenient for you. An amazing learning "listen on the go" experience in a few short minutes—packed with insights and golden nuggets!

BIG DADDY BONUS #3 –
MISUNDERSTOOD!
6 STEPS TO MOVING FROM CONTENTION
TO COMMON GROUND
60 Minute Power-Packed Teleseminar
If workplace clashes are causing you ANXIETY, then this teleseminar replay teaches you how to manage DIFFERING viewpoints and CLASHING styles so you can be your best!

Step 1 – Purchase *Misunderstood!* today, then go to www.TheFastGuideToCommunicatingAtWork.com

Step 2 – Enter your name, email and special code number and get Instant Access to your FREE Bonuses! Your book's special code is FG1CW410E1

---

www.TheFastGuideToCommunicatingAtWork.com

Made in the USA
Lexington, KY
16 February 2013